The Hope Chest:
A Legacy of Love

by Rebekah Wilson

Hope Chest Legacy
California
2003

A note about Hope Chest Legacy

Our goal is to provide insight, information, experience and helpful advice for anyone interested in hope chests. Please visit our website for items, patterns and kits that will help build or create a special and unique hope chest for someone you love.

www.HopeChestLegacy.com.

ISBN #

Hope Chest Legacy
P.O. Box 1398
Littlerock, CA. 93543
www.HopeChestLegacy.com
HopeChestLegacy@aol.com
(888) 554-7292
2003

First printing June 2003
Second printing: November 2003

Dedicated to

**My husband,
Edward...**
who is my best friend, my hero,
my knight-in-shining-armor,
and my dearest love,

**My children,
Rachel, Mary, Kaitlyn, Ezekiel, Isaiah, Uriah & Luke,**
your sweet endearing spirits and unfaltering love
continually inspire my "mommy heart" to greater heights,
you are God's love made visible,

**and In Memory of My Parents,
Edwin and Gladys Keen,**
who made Christ a real and welcome person in our
childhood home,
may your legacy continue on...

Acknowledgments

Writing a book seemed like such an easy idea at first. Had I known all that was involved at the very beginning, this book would still be safely stored in my mind with "future project" stamped all over it. But God in His wisdom shows only what you need to see at any given time. It is not until you are well on your way and you glance back over your shoulder to see how far you have come, that you realize how much you have accomplished and the barriers you have overcome with His help...and you stand in awe and amazement!

I would like to thank the following people for their help and encouragement while researching, writing and compiling the text and final draft of this book — you are SO appreciated...

Renee Blokzyl — for her shared passion in hope chests and needlework and her friendship and encouragement over the last three years.

Carmon Friedrich — for her willingness to edit the whole book on short notice and her patience with my over-abundant use use of commas.

Heather Idoni — who encouraged me from the very beginning to reach out and and do what I though was impossible, write a book! And for giving me wings to fly out on my own.

And to my family...
...who cooked, cleaned, did the laundry and helped care for each other while I was busy typing away on the computer...

You are ALL amazing!
Phillipians 1:3
"I thank God upon every remembrance of you." KJV

Table of Contents

The Hope Chest:
A Legacy of Love

"A Hope Chest is much more than a wooden box and the treasures hidden within it's depths... The Hope Chest contains the love, hope and dreams parents have for their daughter. This is shown in a very special and physical way with each and every item the parent has searched for, considered, and either accepted or declined. It is not the money that goes into the acquisition of a Hope Chest that will make it special, but the love, time and effort of a parent for their child..."

Rebekah Wilson - Author

Introduction

The Hope Chest. The name brings to mind old-world charm, beauty, serenity and love. We picture a lovely young lady, sitting patiently for hours, sewing and creating beautiful items for her soon-to-be new home. With care and skill, she has set aside only the best linens and household items to be used after her wedding.

Through years of preparation, the young lady has earned the elegance, poise and beauty that shines through her. She has an inner confidence in her abilities to become a wife and manage the home for her husband. Her parents have brought up a well-rounded daughter who will be a blessing to her new family and those she meets. This young lady has a visible love for Christ that daily grows deeper. But how has she, out of all other young ladies, reached this goal so easily?

This young lady has been blessed by the gift of a hope chest. She has had the benefit of this physical item. In to which she has placed all her efforts and dreams. The hope chest is a physical symbol of an unforeseen future.

The parents of the young lady helped funnel her energy into learning necessary skills and preparing items to place into the chest for her future. Through her fingers, and the love and nurturing of her parents, the young lady has far more than a chest filled with lovely items waiting for her new home. She has the inner strength, knowledge and ability to handle whatever life sends her way. The hope chest has not only prepared her with physical items for her future, but with mental, emotional and spiritual strengths as well.

The preparation took many years, but because it was an enjoyable process and created many memories for both the young lady and her family, it seemed but a short time before all was made ready.

Any young lady today can be equally blessed through the gift of a hope chest and the skills taught to her while she is still young. In youth, the heart and mind are open and willing to learn new things, and this is the seedtime for the harvest to come. Keeping a child's hands busy, her heart full of love and memories, her mind intent on what God's word tells us...allows that child to grow up pure in a world of chaos and self-ishness. Whether your child has a "physical" hope chest or a small cardboard box to start with, it's the actual process of preparing that builds the inner strength and knowledge that a child needs and will use.

Take the time, help funnel your daughter's energies and heart into her future. You will find that you are enjoying yourself as much as your daughter, and you are making priceless memories in the process...take the time!

My Hope Chest

My father was a wonderful carpenter, and working with wood was truly his gift in life. When I was thirteen, he made my hope chest, and I was allowed to help him. His workshop was our garage, and it was a haven of wood smells and sawdust and tools of every shape, size and description.

To this day, I still have a very vivid memory of helping him hold the sides of my hope chest together as he glued and nailed the end pieces on, and I watched in wonder as all the many pieces came together to form a large beautiful box that was ever so slowly evolving into a priceless treasure.

Although he could not afford the expensive oak, maple or cherry wood that he loved to work with, he built my hope chest out of love... using 1/4 inch thick plain pine plywood and pine wood stock for the trim.

He traced and cut the trim using the scalloped bottom of our kitchen cabinets as a pattern. There is a piano hinge across the back for easier opening and closing, and he bought beautiful white pillowed padding for the inside. With his wisdom, he could foresee items like my wedding veil and crocheted afghans being snagged, so he took the time to cut, fit and glue the padding in.

The Hope Chest

My father also saw a need for small shelves as well, to hold my little treasures, which would otherwise have fallen and been lost at the bottom of the chest. He made two drawers that not only slid back and forth on thin wooden runners nailed along the sides of the chest, but could be lifted out for easier accessibility to the things below.

Together we went to the hardware store and looked over all the different colors of stain. He liked the lighter-colored ones, and I liked the darker. We agreed on cherry and that is still the color of my hope chest today.

He put an old-fashioned brass key lock on the front, imbedded into the chest, and brass latches on either side of the lock. I only have one key, and it is a very special memory for me, when my father finished my hope chest and rubbed it down for the last time. He turned and handed me the key, grasping and holding onto my hands for several minutes with a smile on his face and a few tears in his eyes. In many ways he handed me the key to my future and silently blessed me in my attempts to be prepared for the day I became a special man's wife.

As you can see, there are many memories just in the making of the hope chest alone. Take the time to make these memories with your daughter. Although it may seem a bother to you now, or you think you don't have the time, in the years ahead it will be a special memory for her and one she will cherish.

Introduction

When my father died in June 1992, my hope chest became even more special to me. His rough, callused work-worn hands had made that chest just for ME. There is never a time that I glance at my hope chest without memories of my father flooding over me. Although it often brings a swift sadness to my heart because I still miss him so much, it brings a comfort too. Love made that chest for me, and Love is what I see every time I look at it. My father created a beautiful legacy for me through my hope chest, and that legacy of Love is continually with me each time I run my hand over its smooth surface or see it from across the room.

My mother also blessed me as she helped me fill my chest. One of the things she gave me was a set of china and silverware for my hope chest. She bought these from the grocery store that had specials during the week. This took her nearly a year for the china and another year for the silverware.

This collection was something that she put a great deal of effort into, and because we had very little money when I was growing up, it was a special treat for my mother and father to see it slowly accumulating in the closet. In her whole life, she had never had a set of matching dishes, so this was one gift she wanted to give to her daughter, and she made it happen for me.

Though the china and silverware may not have been the best on the market like most brides seek after and seldom use, it was collected with patience, sacrifice and love. I cherish those sets above any other, not for their value and cost but for the effort and love involved.

My mother died in 1983 when I was only seventeen years old. I have very few items that belonged to her, but I do have wonderful memories of our time together as a mother and daughter, which are treasures in themselves.

Over my pre-teen and teen years, my mother taught me to sew by hand and machine. I enjoyed this so much that I taught myself how to embroider, crochet, quilt and cross stitch by the time I was eleven. With those skills I slowly began to make and accumulate things for my hope chest on my own. My mother would supply what I needed and help when I had trouble. Over time I was able to make crocheted baby afghans, quilts for cribs and large beds too, crocheted doilies, embroidered pillowcases and kitchen towels, pot holders and aprons, tablecloths, napkins, table runners, and much more.

I also learned how to can and preserve food, and I started to collect recipes that went into a special recipe box inside my hope chest. Along the way little treasures from my childhood and teen years found their way inside, as well as pictures of my family, short stories and poems I wrote and anything I wanted to save to share with my future husband and children.

By the time I was grown, I had stored up many memories, as well as material treasures and items that I would need and use in my future home. When I was married to my dear husband at age twenty-two, I had almost everything I needed to set up a new home. My hope chest had served its purpose and was now to be put to a different use.

When I married, all the china, silverware, linens and other goodies that had been stashed away came out and were put into my new home. In their place, my wedding veil and bridal bouquet, pictures of the wedding and other special items took their place.

As our children came along, their little handprints made in salt dough and the baby dresses they wore to my father's funeral and brother's wedding found their way inside. So many things have found their way into my hope chest...baby scrapbooks, the first squiggly picture each child drew as well as successive pictures over the years, locks of hair taken from their wee little heads and placed in a labeled envelope, memories and mementos of my husband's career and our married life, photographs of the homes we have lived in, pictures of the children as they grew, sheet music the girls have played through the years at their recitals, photos of animals and projects we have had, and the list goes on.

Lord willing, I still have many, many years ahead of me, and will I no doubt run out of room, but those little treasures are treasures for a mother's heart and should not be forgotten. Whereas once my hope chest was filled with hopeful things for my future, now it is being filled with memories of my life.

For my family and my children, the greatest hope chest I can give them is the knowledge they take with them: Bible scripture memorized so if they are without a Bible they still know and remember God's word, proper manners and etiquette and the ability to think of others before themselves. I want to give them the knowledge of how to make things and to improvise, a happy childhood filled with wonderful memories and more. But above all, I want to pass on the ability to be content with where God places them in life.

What goes into a hope chest is a very individual, personal and special gift that takes thoughtful consideration through the years until it is finally ready to be given to a daughter when she is grown. Each child's chest will be unique. It would be wrong for anyone to influence parents in what they want to include in their children's hope chests. I would however, like to give some helpful advice, examples and ideas that will help you get started. Remember that nothing is ever set in stone. You may change your mind several years from now and take something out, or, finally put something in that you have hesitated over for a long time.

You may not even have a hope chest in the full sense of the word, meaning you will not have an actual chest, but a closet or cardboard box that holds these items. And you may find that the chest begins to overflow and you need to find another place to put the larger items. Whatever works for you and your circumstances is what you need to concentrate on, not the materialistic ideal that retail companies would like you to think is necessary. It's not the money you put into your daughter's hope chest, but the love behind it that is the true gift. Don't lose sight of that.

The idea of a wonderful and unique hope chest is to create a chest that is tailor-made for each child by loving parents, not something that is mass produced with everyone following the same list of "to get" items. Every child is unique and different, each child has their own particular personalities, likes and dislikes — to create a special hope chest, it should reflect the priceless individuality of each person.

The Hope Chest

Chapter One
History of the Hope Chest

Long ago, before there were "hope chests" there were dowries. A dowry, going back to biblical times, was the price a groom paid to the bride's family in return for his bride. A young woman was a valuable asset to her family and her family's home, often a hard worker and an integral part of the family unit. When she married and went to live with her husband, her family would need to absorb the loss of their daughter, not only emotionally but physically as well. The "dowry" or "bride price" a groom paid would help the bride's family hire someone to do the work the bride would have done.

> And Jacob loved Rachel; and said, I will serve thee seven years for Rachel thy younger daughter. And Laban said, It is better that I give her to thee, than that I should give her to another man; abide with me. And Jacob served seven years for Rachel; and they seemed unto him but a few days, for the love he had to her.
>
> Genesis 29:18-20

Of course, as the story continues, Leah is replaced at

the wedding and Jacob finds he has been wed to the wrong sister! So in Genesis 30:27 we find Laban saying:

> "...then we will give you the younger one also, in return for another seven years of work."

> KJV

This is one of the best examples of a groom paying a dowry for his bride. Rachel was a hard worker, a shepherdess, for her father. If and when she married, her father Laban would have to replace her with someone hired. Laban knew this, but the price of seven years of hard work from Jacob saw a large increase in Laban's wealth through his flocks. Normally this would have allowed Laban to hire a shepherd in place of his daughter. But Laban was a greedy man who did not keep his promises, and God did not bless him.

Throughout time, the customs and manner of dowries changed. It is not clear at what point in history the tables were reversed. There may have been a father, who, out of desperation paid someone to marry his daughter. Or perhaps a father, worried about the future of his beloved daughter, sent with her a large dowry to make sure she would not want for any comfort in the future. This could have made the civilized world consider and realize the benefit in the bride's dowry being taken with her, instead of the groom paying for her and depleting his wealth and ability to care for her. We don't know how things changed, but they did, and a a new trend was set that has continued until the last century.

Although it is hard to say exactly at what point all this changed, in the centuries after 1000 A.D. references are given that show the bride's family was no longer paid for the bride, but that the bride took with her a "dowry" of either money, material possessions or land...or a combination of the three. This was the common tradition for the more wealthy in society, especially for royalty.

> If Isabella wept in the privacy of her chambers for the loss of her son, she represented the face of an indomitable queen to the world. At the height of her grief, she prepared to surrender another child for the glory and prestige of Spain. Henry VII was still eager for the betrothal of his son and heir, Arthur, to Catalina. The dowry was finally agreed upon: 200,000 crowns, half of which would be paid on the wedding day, 50,000 to be paid six months later and 50,000 within a year, the latter payment made up of 15,000 in cash and jewels and the remainder in plate valued at 35,000 which Catalina was to bring with her.
>
> On Whitsunday, 1499, Catalina and Arthur were married by proxy with the Bishop of Coventry and Lichfield representing the Prince and Dr. Rodrigo de Puebla the Princess. Catalina was nearly fourteen and Arthur thirteen.

The Hope Chest

More recently, a dowry is defined as:

> ...the property that a woman brings to her husband at marriage... as her marriage portion, it is given to the husband to defray the expenses of the family.

Funk & Wagnall Encyclopedia, 1959

Not only was money, gold and jewels included but also property, servants, furniture, bolts of cloth and clothing, spices, animals and other material goods. A dowry long ago was to be used to clothe, feed and care for the bride and groom as well as any children they had, for many years to come. Wealthy families were expected to give a large dowry when their daughters married, and if they did not, they were considered rude, low class, boorish or worse.

It was not uncommon for a man to seek out a "wealthy wife," who could, with her dowry, repair his family's lost fortunes. If the young lady was not physically beautiful, the father could increase the dowry offering in hope of a better match for his daughter. Often a "settlement agreement" would be written up before the betrothal, stating EXACTLY what was included in the dowry. This was a legal and binding document that protected both parties.

It is not hard to imagine how the hope chest idea grew out of the custom of the dowry.

History of the Hope Chest

And what about families that were not wealthy? Although they did not have large portions to send with their daughters, there was still the same thought in the minds and hearts of the parent: to send something that would help the young couple as they started their new life together...often in a home with nothing in it but the married couple themselves!

This is where the hope chest began. It quickly became the symbol of the parents' love and concern for their daughter's future, long before she was of marriageable age. Both the parents' and daughter's "hope" of a happy and fulfilling life were wrapped up in the items that were prepared and carefully packed away in a chest. One day their beloved daughter would leave them and be claimed by another to start a new life together.

For even the poorest of families, there was still hope for their daughter's future. Though they could not afford a chest, they still had a place to store the few items that they were able to set aside for their daughter's marriage, to help ease her into her new home. Usually this place was the bottom drawer in a chest-of-drawers, or the bottom of a trunk.

My father often spoke of his grandmother who, as a child, was allotted the bottom drawer for her "hopeful things." She began to put items in that drawer as young as 6 years of age, and she continued to do so until the day she wed.

Depending on the time period, there were either no stores, or very few to go to, to purchase the items that a young woman would need for her new home. With her mother, family and friends, she would begin to prepare and set items aside for her future home and family. Into the chest would go bedding materials like sheets and pillows, quilts and blankets, baby clothing and diapers and infant blankets, silverware, dishes, pots and pans, herb and flower seeds and sewing supplies. Family treasures would be handed down from mother to daughter, such as a wedding dress, jewelry items or the family Bible.

As the daughter grew up, and she learned how to sew, she would practice by making things for her hope chest. The sheets would be hemmed and embroidered, sometimes lavishly, and the pillows would be filled with the fluffy down feathers that had been saved for years from the plucked chickens, ducks and geese that passed through the kitchen.

History of the Hope Chest

The quilt tops would take long periods of time to finish by hand, and the fabric in poorer homes was often taken from the family's old worn-out clothing. When the top was finished there would often be a "quilting bee" or "quilting circle" where friends of the daughter would come to spend the day quilting the layers together, talking, laughing, eating and telling stories or reading from the Bible.

Embroidered table runners and knitted items, crocheted doilies, baby clothing in different sizes from newborn to toddler, braided rugs, oil lamps, candlesticks, books, family recipes, bags of dried medicinal herbs and unguents, even little bits of money scraped together could be hidden away for extreme emergencies...it was a very individual and unique accumulation that was perfectly suited for the young lady for whom it was being prepared.

> The old-fashioned trousseau was planned by indulgent fathers and zealous mothers to last a lifetime. It included stout linens and embroideries that would give a generation of service without showing signs of wear, laces and brocades intended for household possessions to be handed down from mother to daughter, velvets for winter draperies and sheer fabrics for summer curtains. Even people in modest circumstances felt it their duty to outfit their daughters for marriage so that they would not find it necessary to purchase a napkin or towel for year
>
> The New Etiquette, 1924

The Hope Chest

Through the years, the reason for the hope chest has gradually been forgotten. The wonderful heartfelt love and concern that went into each and every item that was carefully placed within its depths has been replaced with store-bought items that have no real heartfelt value. No longer do parents start thinking ahead for the day their daughter will marry, putting things aside for her new home.

Today's parents will go to the local department store to purchase "gifts" for their daughters, as do family members and friends, when the wedding is imminent...usually items the bride and groom have requested through their bridal registry.

It is rare indeed when a wedding gift is something thought out and either handmade or searched for and given from the heart. The loving tradition of the hope chest is nearly gone...

Traditional Items Found in a Hope Chest

For those who may be interested in a list of items that would have commonly been found in traditional hope chests, I am including a short list. Most of the items in the chest were linens of some kind, things a daughter would work on for years in advance of her marriage, often starting as young as 4 or 5 years of age. Other items would be practical ones like her sewing basket, which she would use to make whatever was needed in her new home. There also would have been large items that may not have fit into a hope chest at all, and quite possibly were not made until the betrothal was announced, such as furniture, spinning wheels and looms, rocking chairs and even the cabin or house itself.

> In parts of the old country, a young wife could not set up housekeeping without a dozen dozens, all neatly marked in embroidery, of each sort of household linen. As she finished the marking (embroidery) she put them away, looking forward to the time when she would be married, in a chest...this was her hope chest... American girls have continued the custom, though their stocks of linen have been less copious.

> Love and Courtship in America, 1946

> Our foremothers came to their wedding day supplied with chests filled with plain and durable linen, of their own weaving and fashioning; bed-linen and quilts and spreads in substantial profusion, but with little in the line of showy outside dress; and their whole after lives were but the expression of the wisdom and good judgment of their beginning.

> What a Young Wife Ought to Know, 1905

> In Poland no girl is allowed to marry until she has made with her own hands certain stuffs

and some clothing for her future husband. Such a ruling would certainly seem a hardship to our American girls, but it could well be adopted so far as the household linens are concerned, for surely every girl could do her share toward the equipment of the new home, and these household necessities are certainly her province.

The Hope Chest by H. E. Verran Company, 1917

The following is by NO means a complete list, and keep in mind that not all traditional hope chests would contain the same items, as each young lady's circumstances would differ. The daughter of a wealthy merchant or plantation owner would bring with her items that would not be found in the hope chest of a farmer or tradesman's daughter. Those living in the city would not have the same needs as those living in the country, and even religion could play a part. What a chest would contain in the 1600's would be different than what it would contain in the early 1900's. There are many variables involved, so I have taken the more common items, and have grouped and listed them below.

Pilgrim Era through the Depression Era

The hope chest during this time period would contain many things that would enable the new bride to make and set up her household. It was not uncommon for a bride to have a large amount of linens and household items stored away in her hope chest, but come into the marriage with only two or three sets of clothing and one pair of shoes if she were fortunate.

Furniture was often given to a newly married couple as a wedding gift, usually handmade by the giver, made specifically to fit their new home. It was not uncommon for close family and friends to provide a large bed, trunks, a kitchen hutch or table with benches or chairs. Often friends of the groom would help him build a home after the betrothal was announced and before the wedding took place, if he had not already secured one.

Cradles were items often handed down from parent to daughter, if the parents had finished using it. Some cradles were known to have held several generations of infants in one long family line. These cradles were made to be large, sturdy and long lasting. It was common for an infant to sleep in one until he was nearly two years of age, before moving into a bed.

The following are practical items or items that would have been made or collected for the sole purpose of being taken by the young lady when she was married between 1600-1900 A.D.

Sewing Basket

Needles, needle case or cushion, thread, yarn, knitting needles, crochet hooks, crochet and knitting patterns (either written or actual samples), quilt and quilting patterns, clothing patterns, woven fabrics, scissors, buttons, snaps or other fastenings, pins, needlework hoops, a sewing bird, emery bag, bod kin, bees wax, measuring tape or yard-stick, etc.

It was not only the actual items in the sewing basket, but the knowledge of how to use them to make needed articles in the home, that was the greatest asset to the sewing basket. Every young lady, whether princess or pauper knew how to use a needle.

Weaving Supplies

Cards for cleaning and fluffing wool, drop spindle or spinning wheel, table loom or barn loom, pattern drafts for the loom, dried flowers for dying yarn or woven fabrics and other weaving items and supplies.

Seeds

Herb, vegetable and flower seeds. The bride may also have been given gifts of plant cuttings, bulbs or seedling trees or roses at the time of her marriage. In pilgrim times many of the seeds came across the sea from Europe to the New World and were cherished possessions. During pioneer times, brides often took seeds from their mothers' gardens out west by covered wagon.

History of the Hope Chest

Recipes

Written recipes would depend on whether the bride could read and write. Some young women not only had the recipes, but whole menus of favored meals written out for her. There were also plain standard recipes that were easily kept in the young lady's mind and used daily such as bread and stew recipes. Since most meals in the less wealthy or frontier homes were made from what was available on a daily basis, most young women were taught to cook using seasonings for specific meats and dishes. In this way, recipes were not necessarily needed since the knowledge of using herbs for flavoring food was taught and remembered.

Bedding, Bedroom and Toiletry

Quilts, embroidered bed sheets, pillows, pillow coverings, feather or straw mattress, woven blankets, brass warming pan (to fill with hot coals and move quickly over the sheets to warm the bedding with), dresser scarves and doilies, flannel towels, braided rugs, mirror, wash basin and pitcher, chamber pot, etc.

Kitchen Items

Washtubs, pots and pans or a large kettle, wooden or pewter or tin or china plates and dishes (trenchers) and mugs, water pitchers or barrels, wooden or pewter eating utensils and cooking utensils (pewter spoons made from "spoon molds" and wooden or horn spoons made by whittling, later steel or silver spoons were available), butter churn and molds, woven napkins (in pilgrim days linen napkins were widely used because utensils were not plentiful and people often ate with their fingers), crocheted or woven dishcloths and towels, braided rugs, assorted cooking attachments and implements for cooking in an open hearth or over a wood cook stove (toasting rack, Dutch oven, reflecting ovens, spits, etc.), salt box, tea set or service whether silver or china, and much more.

Miscellaneous

Assorted baskets, large pieces of furniture including large trunks and rocking chairs, oil lamps, candle holders, candle molds for candle making, dressers, cradle, tables, benches or chairs, braided rugs, quilting frame, sewing machine.

Dried Medicinal Herbs

Herbal remedies were often the only available treatments long ago. Having the dried herbs on hand prior to needing them meant the treatment was readily accessible whenever there was a need. Every home where the knowledge of herbal treatments was used and practiced, would have an apothecary chest or another area for storing medicinal herbs.

Dried Food

Depending on the period of history we are talking about, dried food played an important role. In the early days at Plymouth Colony, dried food kept the people alive through the long winters until they could garden again in the spring. Having a large amount of dried corn and other dried foods, including fruits, was a necessity, and they would have been given as gifts to the new couple to get them through their first winter together. Dried food in the pantry meant the ability to eat when fresh food was scarce. Dried corn, fruit, vegetables and meat were very common items.

Farm Animals

Although farm animals were not a physical part of the hope chest, it was a very important wedding gift that would help to start the couple off in their new life together. If the young couple came from a wealthy family, or the groom was a hard worker and had set money aside as a nest egg, good breeding stock would have been purchased, as well as horses. Often it was the gift of a milk cow and laying hens that would be the beginning of the young couple's farm stock. A pregnant sow or a pair of piglets to be raised for breeding were also considered worthy gifts, as were assorted poultry or sheep. Geese, which have been known to live as long as 100 years of age and lay eggs for over 40 years, were often prized as wedding gifts due to the downy feathers that would provide pillows and feather beds from their offspring.

Personal Items

These would be items such as mirrors, hairbrushes, hair clips, a trousseau (clothing) if affordable, religious articles such as Bibles and prayer or hymn books or a crucifix and rosary, childhood mementos and toys, books, clothing she already possessed or had made specifically for her new home such as an apron or head coverings, and any number of other items.

1900 to Present Day

What would the hope chests of more recent times have held? Here is a brief glimpse. Modernization had just begun, and many items that were formerly unavailable or too expensive were suddenly within reach.

For the little house for two, with perhaps a guest room, the following quantity of household linens can be made sufficient:

History of the Hope Chest

10 sheets	24 dinner napkins
8 pillowcases	2 tea sets
3 spreads	4 centerpieces
2 blankets	2 buffet scarves
2 comfortables	4 dresser scarves
12 hand towels	2 bath mats
6 bath towels	6 dish cloths
6 guest towels	6 glass towels
12 wash cloths	4 table cloths

Of course, if it is possible, a dozen sheets and pillow cases and another spread will give one a comfortable feeling of preparedness for any emergency; but the number of articles listed, together with the pieces that friends will give as engagement and wedding gifts, will prove a good foundation from which to build.

The Hope Chest, by H. E. Verran Company, 1917

Modern Era

Today's young ladies who are fortunate enough to have a hope chest when they are married, may have a mother who herself had a hope chest and knows the value of it. Little bits of the young woman's life would have been saved within the depths of the hope chest, as well as family heirlooms from loved ones who have passed away, and items that a mother would have bought and set aside for her daughter.

The Hope Chest

Unfortunately, for most new brides and their parents, they assume the bridal registry covers the area that a hope chest once did. In some ways the bridal registry does do this, by providing the materialistic aspect of the hope chest. Unfortunately, these have been over used for decades. Registries have put an end to the dreams and hopes of parents and young ladies, as they once created and set aside one-of-a-kind handmade articles for the future. Instead, the bride's registry list has replaced these cherished items with mass-produced, overly priced, store-bought items.

The vibrant colorful era of the hope chest and all it stood for has been watered down through mass-produced-factory made items to nothing more than an "itemized shopping list" from the bride.

The Modern Hope Chest

A hope chest is a way for parents to prepare for their daughter's future in a physical way. This is as true today as it has been throughout history...maybe even more so in this modern materialistic world that often scorns parental love and family history and looks down on the thoughts and cares of parents towards their children.

A hope chest is much more than the items that are placed inside, and though it would be easy to provide a complete list of items to fill the chest, there would be no real effort or love involved. A hope chest is the hope and the love that a parent shows physically for their daughter through each and every item that is carefully thought of, created or looked for, and which slowly evolves into the collection of material things for her future.

It is never too late to give your daughter a hope chest, even if she is already married with children of her own! A blessing is a blessing, whether given years ago or in the next few months.

I feel the Lord leading me to prepare for each daughter and her future in a physical way. Compared to the parents of long ago, I have different priorities for my children. What their hope chests will include will have some similarities, but they will also be quite different than the traditional items. I want to send with my children the tools and information they may one day need, as well as "gifts of love" that can help them look back and remember their childhood.

A word of caution here is prudent. Although many companies are starting to resurrect the idea of the hope chest, it is more often than not materialistic in the way it is approached. These companies don't seem to realize the incredible blessing that loving parents can bestow on their daughters, with just a little thought and prayer, through the gift of a hope chest and the items inside.

If the Lord leads you to begin a hope chest for your daughter, one that will be filled with items that you have hand-picked and prayed about, ones that will bless her as a young bride and later as a grandmother, then I hope you will find help, ideas and encouragement throughout this book.

Acquiring A Special Hope Chest

Whether your family builds a hope chest for each child, or you take the time to shop with them in stores or on the internet to find the "perfect chest," it is the thought behind the gift that should be uppermost in the heart and mind.

If you are not handy with woodworking and carpentry and don't want to attempt making one on your own, but you have the desire for your daughter's hope chest to be handmade especially for her, I would suggest finding a friend, relative, neighbor or someone from church who would be willing to either help you make it or do it themselves. You and your daughter would still be able to help by picking out the type of wood you would like, the color of stain or paint, the size and even the design to some degree.

Perhaps there are space restrictions in your home, and there is no possible way to have an actual chest in your child's room. Don't give up! A special place can be found to put away all the items, whether they are in a cardboard box or a drawer or a closet. If you want to give your daughter a chest when she marries, as a wedding gift, you can place all the items you have set aside for her inside the chest as a very special blessing for her.

History of the Hope Chest

If you have financial restraints and cannot afford a hope chest right now, I would urge you to still keep the thought in your heart and your mind, and pray about what you can set aside, even in a shoe box, for your daughter. Over the years you may fill one shoe box and move on to another and another and even bigger and bigger boxes. The small amount of time, effort and sacrifice you make now will be a wonderful investment in your daughter's future, and she will see the time, thoughtfulness, and effort that went into your gift.

When you have decided on an item to include in your daughter's hope chest, you will also need to decide whether you will actually put it "in" the hope chest or if you will need to package it carefully and place it in a closet or in another place to keep safe.

When my mother bought my silverware, it was placed in my hope chest. When my china began to accumulate, it would not all fit inside. So we had a closet that was allotted for the china and other large items. You may find that this happens to you too; don't be discouraged if you have accumulated so many things that they won't all fit. It will be a huge blessing later!

If you have more than one child you are saving items for, and you are using the same area as an overflow for items that won't fit into their chests, take a few moments to mark the items for each child. A little scrap of paper pinned to the item can be a great investment in later years. If something were to happen and they were left without you to divide the items into each child's hope chest, it could prove to be a very hard task for them to do. Also, as the years pass, you may actually forget whose item is whose! Take a few moments now, and it will be a great help in future years.

The Bridal Registry

At the turn of the century, factories and large retail stores began to replace the homemade items found in many homes. By 1940 it was acceptable for the bride to "register" at retail stores and create a list of the items she would like to receive as wedding presents. Though this may seem practical to a large number of people, in many ways it put an end to the era of the hope chest and gift giving from the heart. Instead of thought and effort, either in the making or collecting of a gift or seeking after an object to give as a heartfelt offering, it allowed the lazy giver to quickly purchase an object that held little or no meaning in the presentation of the gift. There were no heartstrings attached, no real effort put into the acquisition of the gift, and more often than not the gift itself was mass produced and would be easily replaced if lost or damaged.

Since the advent of the bridal registry starting around 1940's, the wedding gifts that a bride "requests" are often for very expensive items that a wedding guest often feels pressured into purchasing. Since guest does not want to disappoint or offend the bride and groom, large amounts of money are spent on items that may never actually be used by the new couple. Retail stores understand the situation perfectly and use it to their advantage. Instead of asking what the bride will "need" for her new home, she is asked what she "wants" while she is walking through the store and being shown the best china, crystal, and most expensive sets of sheets and towels and household items. Though these things are certainly beautiful, and there may be brides out there who would actually use them, for most new couples the reality is they will seldom, if ever, use the expensive china and crystal they receive. Those items will only collect dust sitting in a china hutch and receive occasional glances. Years later the couple often cannot remember who the gift giver was without looking it up in their wedding book.

Often, the most appreciated gift is the one given from the heart. With every glimpse, it brings the giver to mind. The crocheted afghan from Grandmother, the embroidered pillowcases and matching sheets from a dear aunt, a quilt created by several close friends using the bride's favorite colors, a set of dishes for everyday use from a church member, family china handed down from mother-in-law to her new daughter-in-law, and so on. With thought and effort, there should be very little need for a bride to register at retail stores, and it should be with the idea in mind that guests who do not know the couple, and may have a hard time finding an appropriate gift, would be the ones to use the registry.

The Hope Chest

Mom did give EACH granddaughter china, good quality china that will last the entire life of the couple, BUT bought it and has been buying patterns from antique stores and thrift stores for years for this purpose. The old stuff is better she says...

Renee Blokzyl

A bridal registry does have its place, but it needs to be thought of as a "help" and should not be used for the accumulation of items that will have little use in the home. Instead, the bride should think of practicality. What will she need and use on a DAILY basis? With what will she want to decorate her home? It will not do if she has a beautiful set of china that she is afraid to use for fear of breaking it and no everyday dishes for her table. Or a beautiful linen bedspread that needs to be dry-cleaned, instead of a quilt or coverlet that can be easily washed in the washing machine.

When presenting a gift to someone, it should not be the amount of money spent on the gift that shows how much love the giver has for the recipient, but the thought, time and effort that went into the acquisition of the gift that shows the recipient they are well-thought of and loved. Time is far more precious that any amount of money! A gift given from the heart far more precious than something picked from a bridal registry list.

History of the Hope Chest

"Emerson says: "Our tokens of love are for the most part barbarous, cold and lifeless, because they do not represent our life. The only gift is a portion of thyself. Therefore let the farmer give his corn; the miner his gem; the sailor coral or shells; the painter his picture, and the poet his poem."

To persons of refined nature, whatever the friend creates takes added value as part of themselves - part of their lives, as it were, having gone into it. People of the highest rank, abroad, will often accept, with gratitude, a bit of embroidery done by a friend, a poem inscribed to them by the author; a painting executed by some artist; who would not care for the most expensive bauble that was offered them. Mere costliness does not constitute the soul of a present; it is the kind feeling that it manifests which gives it its value. People who possess noble natures do not make gifts where they feel neither affection nor respect, but their gifts are bestowed out of the fullness of kind hearts.

Our Deportment by John Young, 1881

The Hope Chest

At my first bridal shower, six weeks prior to the wedding, I opened a package to find three sets of hand-embroidered pillowcases, or pillow slips as Nannie called them. Beautifully starched, they were all white, embroidered in white, with wonderful satin stitching, beautiful French knots, detailed rosettes cascading all over each and every one. The hours of work that had to go into each one! And I had *three* sets!

I did at that time, and still do, love to sew. I had also done some cross-stitching and counted cross-stitch as well as crocheting. But I had never seen such beautiful stitching in anything before. I was almost speechless. Nannie just smiled and said that she hoped I enjoyed using them.

For our wedding gift, she gave us two pillows she had hand embroidered in crewelry, using wool yarns. Nannie had chosen the colors to match our mis-matched living room furniture. Being newlyweds and my husband just graduating from college, we had no money to speak of to spend on new furniture, so we had hand-me-downs from family members. They all kind of meshed together in those 70's colors that are so atrocious to see now! But Nannie's pillows somehow pulled them all together.

So, you see, when I use Nannie's pillowcases or any of her handwork that we have, it's like she's still here with us. Her stitches remind me of her love and desire to give something of herself to our future. She is still participating in our lives, in our joys and our trials. And, in years to come, when our children marry and leave home, Nannie will still be there with them and their children as well, connecting her past with their present.

Merri Williams

Here is a common list of modern items and the numbers requested by brides when they register for wedding gifts through several of the larger retail stores.

Fine China: 8-12 place settings with all additional items to complete the china set

Casual China: 8-12 place settings with all additional items to complete the china set

Stemware

Barware

Sterling Flatware: 8-12 place settings with all the additional items to complete the set

Stainless Flatware: 8-12 place settings and all the additional items to complete the set

Frames and Vases

Serving Trays and Bowls

Housewares Dinnerware: 20 piece sets or 8-12 place settings and all additional items needed to complete set

Houseware Glassware: same quantity as your china**Houseware Flatware:** 2- 20 piece sets or 45 piece set

The Hope Chest

Houseware Accessories
- measuring cups and spoons
- mixing bowls
- utensils
- dishtowels and dishcloths
- hot pads
- canister set

Electric Items:
- mixer
- skillet and waffle iron
- bread maker
- rice cooker
- toaster or toaster oven
- food processor
- blender and juicer
- coffee and tea makers

Cookware:
- sauce, sauté, omelet, frying pans
- stockpot or Dutch oven
- tea kettle
- double boiler
- wok
- roasting pan
- casserole dishes

Bakeware:
- casserole dishes
- roasting and muffin pans
- cake and pie pans
- pizza, baking and bread pans

Cutlery: complete set of paring, chef, bread, carving, cleaver, slicing and steak knives and knife sharpener

Table Linens: placemats, napkins and rings, tablecloths

Bed Linens:
- pillow cases and shams (6 each)
- flat and fitted sheets (6 each)
- mattress pads
- bed skirts
- blankets
- comforters
- pillows

Bath and Toiletry:
- bath and hand towels (6 each)
- washcloths (6 each)
- bath rugs
- shower curtains, rings and liners

Luggage

As you can see, today's wedding gifts are very materialistic and easily replaced and it is an unusual gift giver who is brave enough to give something from the heart. A hope chest that has been slowly created over the years of your daughter's upbringing can be that special gift.

The Hope Chest

Chapter Two
What Belongs in a Hope Chest?

The following is a list of ideas for items you may want to consider for your child's hope chest. This is not a complete list by any means. Remember it is a legacy you are giving your daughter, and it should come from your heart through searching, discarding and finally having a peace about what is included and given to each child. There are no right or wrong items to include or not include, it all comes down to your heart's choices. Your individual preferences and selections are what makes each hope chest so special and so different from all others.

Family Heirlooms

> Some of my heirlooms are very old; others are rather new. What makes them an heirloom to me is that someone I loved and was related to once owned it, made it, or gave it to me, and it cannot be duplicated."
>
> Peggy A

Are there any special family heirlooms that have been handed down to you through your mother,

mother-in-law, grandmother or other special people in your life? Do you have any heirlooms you have acquired through your lifetime and would like to pass down to your daughter?

> I have my grandmother's special prayer book she compiled with well loved prayers, beautiful photos, etc. My grandfather had a special prayer he said each and every day as soon as he got out of bed, on his knees next to the bed. He wrote it down and gave it to me...I treasure that piece of paper!
>
> I have found that through the years, I treasure more items with barely any value...just because they offer a memory that I hold dear to my heart.
>
> Renee Blokzyl

Handing down family heirlooms was once a common tradition, but slowly, throughout the last few generations, the tradition has been lost. Instead of family history and values being passed down through many generations by the personal articles of loved ones, this modern age has embraced the materialistic tendency to buy items that hold no strings to the heart and are easily replaced. It is not surprising that the moral values of the past are being lost, and generations raised today have no ties to bind them to their families.

Grandmother's lace hanky or Grandfather's gold

watch were once reminders of personal values and family strengths and commitments. Just the sight of those family heirlooms can give a sense of strength and self-worth, and they remind the young person that there is responsibility in life and to value it.

> I had a necklace when I was in my twenties that my grandmother asked to wear for a season to a special place she was traveling (Canada to my cousin's for a few weeks one year). She gave it back to me later, and I wore it another 15 years before passing it along to our daughter, who wears it now. My grandmother never asked me for anything but that borrowed necklace, so it was a treasure to me that she wore it, and allowed me to loan it to her...

> I have one of my Dad's baby-shoes from about 1920. Button-up leather booties for a just walking little boy! I also have one of my shoes, and one pair each from our children. Little treasures!

> I have an old, inexpensive brooch of my Mom's that I remember her wearing when I was a young teenager. I wear it now, in honor of Mom.

> Joan Taylor

Consider reviving the tradition of family heirlooms. Give your daughter a special family heirloom that will remind her of someone she loves and respects. This does not need to be expensive. In fact, some of the most treasured heirlooms are often ones that have no real material value, only sentimental value. Small pieces of costume jewelry, articles of clothing, pictures or photos, small trinkets, letters, sewing accessories, one plate from a family set to place on her wall or in her china hutch, a teacup that someone dear used, journals from grandparents. Nearly anything can be a family heirloom, even locks of hair as this mother wrote:

> One of our most prized possessions are my mother's braids! My grandmother would not let my mother cut her hair until she reached her freshman year in high school. The reason was probably that my grandmother felt shorter hair was for older girls. Anyway, my mother always kept her long hair in two braids. The day she was allowed the grown-up hair cut, my grandmother first cut off the two long braids in their kitchen and then sent my mother off to the beauty shop. My grandmother kept the braids, gave them to my mother who gave them to me. My mother went to be with the Lord seven years ago now, and those braids are precious to us. The unique thing about them though is that the hair is still as soft as when grandma cut them off.

> Debbie Phelps

One mother I know had been given several large pieces of furniture, some kitchen items and an old antique juicer when her husband's grandmother moved from a large home into a smaller apartment. Although they kept the furniture, this mother didn't have any need for the kitchen items, so she gave them to someone else, who was happy to accept them and planned on placing the items, especially the antique juicer, in her own daughter's hope chest. This caused the first mother to wonder if she should have kept them, to save them for her own daughters, but she had never considered the idea before, and it was too late.

Take the time while the items are IN YOUR HANDS to decide if they are something that should be kept or discarded. Once they are gone there is no way to retrieve it. It is also a good idea to request that any items promised to children or grandchildren be put into writing or in the person's will. Although this may be awkward, it may help avoid any problems in the future. Having lived through this with my father's death and a step-mother who was very angry at the world and jealous of her step-children, it will be a safeguard for your children and will allow them to receive items that were meant for them.

If you have items that have been in the family for years, write a note or index card that can be left with the item. This does not need to be fancy by any means, just a little note with as much information as possible about the item. Include the history behind it, who has owned it, used it or worn it, and what it means to the family. Any information on the item at all should be written down, even if the whole story is not complete...something is better than nothing.

The Hope Chest

My mother-in-law's great-grandmother (my dear husband's great, great-grandmother) was baptized in a special christening gown. It was from Belgium, made by some nuns there in a convent approximately 130 years ago. It featured batiste cotton, lots of Brussels lace and French laces. Over time it has been lovingly kept in blue tissue paper to preserve it, and some of the ribbons have been replaced several times since. It now resides in Holland and won't be coming back to North America because all the other cousins want to use it now for their little ones.

Renee Blokzyl

Following are several ideas that you can consider if you do not have any heirlooms to pass down, but, of course, following your heart is the best gift. These are only suggestions, and with some thought you can adapt them or come up with many, many more!

Adopting Antique Items

With the thought in your mind of handing something of value down to your daughter and future grand-daughters, you can look through antique stores and thrift shops to find antique items that you can incorporate into your family life. Whole sets of china can be bought from thrift and antique stores. Candlesticks can be used as a decoration and can also be set on the table during special occasions to make memories. Tea cups, whether matching or from different sets, can be used at mother-daughter tea parties. These cups will become special heirlooms that can be passed on to grandchildren. Memories of these kinds of items will create their own special place in your daughter's heart, and she will treasure the items you have "adopted."

Other items you might want to consider are: jewelry (either expensive or costume), quilts, tea pots or tea sets or special tea cups, serving spoons, paintings, hand-sewn samplers, hand-crocheted items, perfume bottles, china, dolls, trinket boxes, cookie cutters, silverware, crystal dishes, sugar bowls, canister sets, crocheted doilies, furniture, lamps, picture frames...just about anything that you can bring into your home and use can be bought with the thought of sending it with your daughter as part of her hope chest.

Creating and Using an Item Solely to be Used and Handed Down

Sounds intimidating, doesn't it? It shouldn't be. Whether simple or complex, this can be a fun family time of brainstorming for ideas.

The Hope Chest

For my eldest daughter's wedding, I dug out my sewing machine and created several heritage French sewing clothings, but the sweetest thing to me that I made were two little ring bearer pillows I created for the rings. These were made for two little boys to carry...with 18 sections of lace, ruffled batiste, entredeux, Swiss ribbon embroidery, etc...all sewn together to create the tops, silk ribbon to use for ties, etc.

I gave one to my daughter to keep and now the other one is for all my other children to use for their weddings. I will simply change the color of the silk ribbon to match their own special choosings. They have all commented on using it.

I've also made a baptismal gown and a First Communion dress with batiste and lots of French lace that my children have worn. I embroider their names on the slips inside with the date they wore them for heirloom quality too. I will also embroider all the wedding dates and names on the pillow bottom opening.

Renee Blokzyl

Some Simple Ideas

One simple idea is a special birthday cake plate that is used for each and every birthday that is celebrated. This can be plain glass or crystal, or one made of clay you allow the children to paint with permanent paints. By using this special cake plate, you are making your own family memories and traditions that will mean a great deal years from now. There may be some who think this would become annoying or a burden, no one needs to do this. If you do, remember that just by using the plate, you are giving a gift of memories and family tradition to your children.

Along this same line is the "You are Special Today" plate. There are companies that sell these plates, or you can make one yourself. Buy a plain clay or china plate and use paints that are safe for food dishes (look in your local craft store), and make your own. Write "You Are Special Today" or "You Are SUCH a Blessing" on the plate, or any other saying you would like, and either decorate it or leave it plain with just the wording visible.

I even know of one family that will write on the back with a permanent paint pen the date it was used EVERY time they bring it out. When one plate is used up, they move onto a new plate. Over time they have created a unique set of special plates filled with family memories.

This "special" plate can be used for any occasion, from celebrating a special event in the life of a family member to just cheering someone up if they have had a hard day. Imagine your daughter's joy when she goes through her hope chest and finds this wrapped and waiting for her to make her own memories with! Or if you have more than one daughter, instead of handing down "The Plate," make one for each daughter and hide it in her hope chest. The thoughts and the memories she has of how the family used the "Special Plate" will inspire her to begin this tradition in her new home.

If you decide to start this tradition in your home, consider using a plastic plate if you have a large family with small children. Once it's been "lovingly worn out," and the children are old enough to be trusted not to break it, allow the plastic one to retire to a nice place on the wall or in the cupboard, and start fresh with a nice glass, clay, crystal or china plate.

Purchasing a set of candlesticks that can be used for special occasions or once a week during "Family Night" can be an easy and inexpensive memory maker. When you bring these out, let the children take turns lighting them. This is something they will look forward to and will be a special way of creating memories. The glow of a candle is soothing and calming and brings comfort and security into a home. Including a pair of candlesticks in your daughter's hope chest can be a sweet reminder of the times she shared with her parents at home, especially if her memories cover many years.

Look in thrift stores or antique stores for some very nice and often inexpensive candlestick sets. Make an effort to start using them for special times or holidays, and the memories will take care of themselves.

Are there any family traditions that you have that can be turned into a physical item for the hope chest?

What Belongs in a Hope Chest?

For example, a certain Bible passage that is read on Christmas Eve or over the turkey at Thanksgiving? A special prayer that your daughter learned and recited every night when she was young? A favorite family saying that is well known and loved? A favorite family hymn? Consider asking someone with calligraphy skills or beautiful writing to write this out on parchment paper, and have it framed. For my daughters I am using cross stitch and embroidery to create a special remembrance for them of Bible verses we have shared over the years, or something else that has touched us, and I will have these professionally framed for them.

What about family picnics that you go on at certain times of the year? Have you thought of creating a picnic basket for your daughter that she can use while she is courting, betrothed and later with her own family? A sturdy basket and unbreakable dishes and silverware can, with care, last through your grandchildren.

One of our family traditions that I am turning into a physical gift is cookie cutters. We make lots of cookies. Sugar cookies, gingerbread cookies or any cookie where the dough is rolled out and cut are special favorites with my children: gingerbread men, gingerbread houses, ginger bears, sugar people and sugar flowers, maple leaves and more. I have started to collect an assortment of recipes and cookie cutters. Some of the cutters are steel, others are copper and plastic. I have also started to save the jar lids that we use for plain round sugar cookies. I have these stored in a box, and we use them continually. One day they will be divided up among my children for my grandchildren to enjoy. There is a wonderful company that sells hundreds of different cookie cutters, which you will find listed in the appendix of this book.

We enjoy flowers, and three flowers in particular grow well here in our desert area. The morning glory springs up from the ground year after year, with little or no help from us. The four-o'-clock blooms daily and survives even the hottest of days with no damage to its leaves or flowers. The sweet pea is always a welcome addition year after year and makes even the most drab area of the yard beautiful.

My daughters love these flowers, and they are always eager to run out and see how many are open and what colors have appeared since they were out in the yard the day before. It's also a family tradition to gather as many seeds from these flowers as possible during the summer and fall months and save them for the following year. Many happy hours have been spent outside gathering the seeds and talking to each other. We often send our seeds along in letters and Christmas cards for friends and relatives too, so they can enjoy "our" flowers in their own yards.

My mother told me that when her grandmother married she took with her seeds from her mother's herb and flower gardens as a starting stock for her own garden. This was a common practice long ago. The pioneers would take treasured seeds and plant cuttings or bulbs from the east coast all the way to the west. When they were planted, those seeds, cuttings and bulbs reminded them of their old home that was now so far away.

Seeds up until the 1940's were the heirloom type, not the hybrid variety found today. Heirloom seeds can be collected from mature plants, dried and planted with a very good success rate on growth. With today's hybrid variety, we are not able to do that any longer. Hybrid seeds do not reproduce well, and if they do are poor plants or have very low growth and reproduction rates. This is one reason why gardeners today need to buy new seed every year. There are still many plants, like the morning glory, marigold, cosmos, sweet pea's, four-o'-clock and others, that retain the heirloom reproductive quality. These seeds can be saved and given to your daughter. There are several seed catalogs that specialize in heirloom seeds, and there are books on how to collect and save the seeds.

One gift that my daughters will receive is the seeds from the morning glory, sweet peas and four-o'-clock plants that we enjoy so much. These plants have graced our garden and fence with beauty throughout the springs and summers of my daughters' youth. This is a simple, low cost link to their childhood, and one that my daughters will truly enjoy.

Plant cuttings are another wonderful way to pass on family heritage and a love for flowers and plants. This is very easily done and blesses the young lady with memories and beauty in her new home. This would be something that would need to be given after her wedding, so the cuttings would not perish. There are a wide number of plants that are good for this, geraniums being the most common and hardy of the plants. Geraniums can also be planted in pots and placed indoors to bloom throughout the year.

One young lady I knew as a child, had been raised on the east coast. When her husband was transferred to the west coast, her mother and grandmother took flower cuttings, seeds and flower bulbs from their gardens and gave them to her for her new home, as a remembrance of her family. These same plants have grown in her yard ever since. Through several different moves she always carefully took cuttings, saved seeds and dug bulbs to take with her.

Several years ago she received a phone call that her grandmother had been rushed to the hospital and was dying. In tears the granddaughter went out to her flower garden and knelt on the ground in prayer. Surrounded by the flowers her grandmother's hands had once touched and tended years ago, she was able to find peace and accept that the Lord was calling her grandmother home.

Not long after, when her own daughter married and started a small window garden in the tiny apartment that she and her husband rented, her mother brought a housewarming gift of plant cuttings, seeds and flower bulbs.

What Belongs in a Hope Chest?

This was the fourth generation that was blessed by flowers from the same stock, and I have no doubt that this beautiful heritage will be passed on to the future generations in that family.

> My mother's backyard is almost like a temple to me, as she's bathed the garden there in her prayers and tears for years as she's tended it and prayed for her family. It's where she escapes to when she's troubled or burdened, and seeks the Lord. I've asked for cuttings from her garden, and those plants in our garden are precious to me as they remind me of Mama and the Lord.
>
> Joan Taylor

The Hope Chest

Books

Few mothers can over-estimate the influence which the companionship of books exerts in youth upon the habits and tastes of their children, and no mother who has the welfare of her children at heart will neglect the important work of choosing the proper books for them to read, while they are under her care. She should select for them such as will both interest and instruct, and this should be done during the early years, before their minds shall have imbibed the pernicious teachings of bad books and sensational novels. The poison imbibed from bad books works so secretly that their influence for evil is made greater than the influence of bad associates. The mother has it in her power to make such books the companions and friends of her children as her good judgment may select, and to impress upon them their truths, by conversing with them about the moral lessons or intellectual instructions they contain. A taste may be easily cultivated for books on natural science and for history, as well as for those that teach important and wholesome lessons for the young.

Our Deportment by John Young, 1881

We are a family of readers, and books are a very vibrant part of our family life. My book lists will undoubtedly change throughout the years ahead, as we come across other books that impact our lives. For this reason I have an ongoing list for all my children, of book titles specifically chosen for them.

Each child is unique and has specific book favorites that she will enjoy reading again at some future point. The titles, the number of books and reason I include a book will vary. The books I feel led to give my children may not fit your daughter's needs or likes, so please accept any titles as examples only.

Since we are a family who enjoys good books, one of the choices for our daughter's hope chest would naturally be books, especially books that we have shared as a family or that she has enjoyed sometime in her life. Many families are not book lovers, and their choices in this area will be very different. Consider what your daughter would enjoy or possibly need, and if you feel led to place books in her hope chest, you can start an ongoing list.

What I have found helpful in my pursuit of books to include in the hope chest, and deciding when to spend the money on them, is to make a list for each child. This list includes the book titles, authors, publishers and copyright dates of each book I am considering. This is a long list. With prayer, I am led to the ones that I know are right for each child, and I will purchase the books when possible.

If I am unable to find a book, I place a star next to it so I remember that it is a book to keep searching for. It is very rewarding to check books off the list, hoping that my children will appreciate each choice someday in the future.

The Hope Chest

We can use the same reasoning for movies or books on tape as well. What is available now, and your daughter enjoys, may not be available when she is grown and has children of her own with whom to share them. By spending a little extra time now, you can provide your daughter with a link to her childhood that she can share with her own children one day. This can be so easily overlooked, but is actually a simple thing to do, and your effort will be rewarded sometime in the future.

Even if I am unable to find the book, tape or video, the list remains. If I were called home to be with the Lord before my children were grown, my husband would still have these lists. If nothing else, they would be a love letter of sorts, from me to my children.

What Belongs in a Hope Chest?

A Family Bible

What better gift can you give your daughter as she begins her new life, than a beautiful new Bible, one with all the family history already inside, written in her mother's or father's own hand? A message from both parents inscribed within is also a special way to show your love for her.

It was once tradition for the bride carry a new Bible down the aisle during her wedding march. This tradition was lost long ago, and few people even know about it any more. If you resurrect this idea, be sure to have the wedding official and wedding party, as well as any witnesses, sign the Bible after the wedding ceremony. It may be your only chance to have all their signatures written down. This would only take a few moments, but years later it will be something that would be cherished.

It would be an added blessing for your daughter if you were able to collect her family and her friends' favorite Bible verses or spiritual testimonies, and place those in a special book or album to go with the Bible. If at all possible, have the people write it down themselves in their own handwriting; it will mean so much more years later, when many will have moved away or have left this earth for heavenly places. Often what someone older and wiser tells us while we are young goes over our heads and is lost. It is not until years later, when we are in the midst of struggles, that we long for those words again. Only those wise ones are gone and all we have left is a vague memory of things they have said. To be able to read it in their own hand when we need it most would be such a blessing! If the relatives or friends are unable to attend the ceremony, or live far away, ask if they can write something down and mail it to you. When it arrives, simply attach it inside the book so it will be included.

I have often longed for a list of my mother's favorite Bible verses and the things she had learned through hard times and many struggles, but I did not have the foresight as a child and teenager to collect and write them down. My mother died when I was seventeen, and her wisdom and love of scripture is gone with her. Take the time to do this for your daughter; you have no idea how much she will one day appreciate it or yearn for it if you don't!

If there are elderly grandparents, relatives or neighbors who have trouble writing, or if there is someone who is handicapped in some way and unable to write, make a tape recording of what they would like to give to your daughter. This is a very precious gift!

There is one more Bible that can be given to your daughter, and one that she will treasure dearly: the Bible that her mother, father or grandparents have read daily, and circled verses in or underlined. One that has been worn through the years and has been cried in and held onto for strength is a precious heirloom.

One elderly woman, during a recent Bible study,

shared how she would specifically buy a Bible that had wide margins. The wide margins allowed her to write notes, dates and thoughts in them. Through the years, as she and the Lord worked though a Bible together, she would write little notes about what was happening in the family, people she prayed for, trials she suffered through and overcame. Anything that touched her was written in small print in the margins of her Bible. Verses were underlined or circled, marks were made throughout the Bible, and it became a personal treasure to be handed down to one of her many children. When one Bible was filled up, she moved on to a new Bible and started over again. In this way she was able to provide a very special and very personal part of herself to her children and grandchildren. It took nearly her entire lifetime to work through enough Bibles to pass one on to each of her children, but each Bible is a living history of her walk with the Lord and those she loved and prayed for. What an incredible insight this dear lady had to prepare for so long a gift that would have such deep meaning to each person who was fortunate enough to receive it! If only we all had the foresight to think ahead in such a way.

My Mother's Bible

This book is all that's left me now,
Tears will unbidden start,

The Hope Chest

With faltering lip and throbbing brow
I press it to my heart.
For many generations past
Here is our family tree;
My mother's hands this Bible clasped,
She, dying, gave it me.

Ah! well do I remember those
Whose names these records bear;
Who round the hearthstone used to close
After the evening prayer,
And speak of what these pages said,
In tones my heart would thrill!
Though they are with the silent dead,
Here are they living still!

My father read this holy book
To brothers, sisters, dear;
How calm was my poor mother's look,
Who loved God's word to hear!
Her angel face - I see it yet!
What thronging memories come!
Again that little group is met
Within the halls of home!

Thou truest friend man ever knew,
Thy constancy I've tried;
When all were false, I found thee true,
My counselor and guide.
The mines of earth no treasures give
That could this volume buy;
In teaching me the way to live,
It taught me how to die!"

George P. Morris

What Belongs in a Hope Chest?

My parents' Bibles had served them throughout their Christian lives. Both Bibles were well-worn and thoroughly covered in multicolored pencil and pen marks and had tiny scribbles in them where notes had been made along the margins. Both Bibles had page tears taped together with scotch tape, which had turned a deep golden color with age. Those Bibles I had seen daily in each of their hands, with my mother's head covering carefully tucked in the back cover of hers. Both Bibles had weathered through their 25 years of marriage and were handed down to their children. My brother has both Bibles, one next to the other where they always were and should always be. But how I long to have them in my hands again as well...

Childhood Books

I have favorite books that I have read at least a dozen times and that I continue to keep because I enjoy them so much. Recently, I was blessed to find a copy of a book I read in third grade that has always been a part of me. I tried to find this book for years, especially when I started to have my own children. What a joy it is to have it now and to be able to read it to my daughters! The enjoyment I had so long ago when I was young is being re-lived through my children because of this book. My daughters are showing the same tendencies I have in re-reading favorite books. My oldest has read one of the Little House books over six times and

STILL enjoys reading it again and again. Although I don't encourage this, I do understand it. There are just some books that become a part of us and we carry them in our hearts forever.

Obviously these favorite books of my daughter's will be included in her hope chest. She has many others that are also favorites and will be included in her chest, but the Little House book is a special one to her. Fortunately this book is still in print, so I was able to get a beautiful hardback copy with a dust jacket for her. As she grows older she may have other books that become special to her, that I will consider finding copies of for her as well.

If a book is out of print (OOP), it may be harder to find, but it is still possible. Because we homeschool and use a "living books" approach to schooling, we are constantly reading and using OOP books. Many of these are quickly becoming family favorites. Our family library is continually growing by leaps and bounds!

To help your efforts in finding those "special" books that your daughter has enjoyed, or perhaps even books that you may have enjoyed and would like to find, I am including several companies and websites in the appendix. These should be helpful in locating hard to find books for sale.

Another good source for hard to find books is eBay. This is a large online auction website at: www.ebay.com. You can do a search for title, author or subject (put "book" in the search to limit then items

items that will be brought up for you). There are several drawbacks to eBay, however. One is that you may not be able to find the book you are looking for one week, but it may be listed over the next several weeks, so be sure to check often. Another drawback is that you may be outbid and lose that hard-to-find book. However, an aspect that draws many buyers to eBay, is that you can often find those hard-to-find items much more inexpensively than you would on a used book website.

> All the living books we read together I keep as treasures to pass along too. The children know which books I've read aloud, and they also know I've set them aside for them to have one day. The entire library we've created will be theirs, and they cherish it already. However, those special books we've read aloud I'm *expected* to keep for them, because our memories of laughing and crying over the story are so crisp. They have asked that I not sell those books, or substitute another for the one I actually read (dog-eared, tattered or falling apart...doesn't matter!)
>
> Joan Taylor

Another item to include is a baby book your child enjoyed while a toddler. I have several of my daughters' favorite picture books set aside, ones that they enjoyed as toddlers or small children, so they can share those memories with their own children. I also keep an ongoing list of book titles we have read aloud as a family. When my children are grown, they can go through and remember those stories, or use the list for book suggestions to read aloud with their own children.

How many favorite books I end up including in my daughters' hope chests will vary, as will the books themselves. There is no set list that each child will have, but instead I want this to be as personal as I can make it, tailor fit for each child.

As a special addition to each book selected, I write an inscription on the inner cover and include the date the book is given or placed aside for that child. It usually goes something like this,

> Dearest _____, this was once your favorite picture book when you were 2 years old. I hope this still carries many wonderful memories for you, and you can create new memories with your own children. Love Mom & Dad

- or-

> Dearest _____, I have many fond memories of your nose glued to the pages in this book when you were 10 years old. I hope it still brings you joy! Love Mom & Dad

If there is a favorite book that your whole family has enjoyed but is very hard to find, or if there are favorite picture or story books that your daughter has really enjoyed, consider reading these aloud and recording them onto tape for your grandchildren to listen to. There are a few tricks to this, but it is basically a very simple thing to do and one that will be appreciated many years from now.

My husband has recently started to record specific books onto tape so our children can listen throughout the day. Many of these books are ones our family has either enjoyed numerous times before, or the books are a part of our schooling. Young children especially, can listen while someone reads to them and still learn and retain a large amount of what they have heard. Whether my children can read for themselves or not, by recording these books onto tape my husband is able to help read to the children when I am too busy. These are a big favorite with my children, and they often listen over and over and over again to the same book.

When my husband is done with a book, it is a very simple thing to make several extra copies and tuck them away for my children's children. Once again, by taking the time to do these little things, you are investing in the future happiness of loved ones.

There are a few tricks to recording books onto tape, and I will give some hints here. Only attempt to do this when the house is quiet, so there is no background noise competing with your voice. Purchase a cheap microphone; the small expense does pay off with a better recording in the end. When you are ready to start, try reading aloud for several minutes before you start to record, this helps warm up your voice and get your reading rhythm going. Then go back to the beginning and start to record yourself reading. The first time you record, try holding the microphone at several different distances from your mouth while you are recording. After several minutes of recording, rewind the tape and listen to see which distance works best for sound quality.

We have found that the readers mouth should be two inches away from the microphone...too close and the words are jumbled and overly loud. If it is too far away, it sounds like the voice is fighting its way through deep water to be heard.

Try reading a set number of pages; we use ten pages. Time yourself to see how fast you read aloud. It is fairly easy to figure out how many pages you read per minute, multiply that by the number of pages in the book, and you will be able to figure out how many tapes you will need or what lengths should be used for the best overall finished product. You can purchase tapes in lengths of 30, 45, 60, 90, or 120 minutes per tape. Once all of this has been done, rewind the tape and start making memories for your children and grandchildren!

> My eldest daughter loved to make tapes for her brothers and sisters. She made one for a Christmas gift then one again for our summer vacation to entertain everyone on our long drives. We still have these tapes today...six in all and it's real fun to listen to them and fondly remember those giggles over the noises she enhanced the

stories with.

This daughter is now 24 with her own babe so they will be copied for her family to cherish. She would take several favorite books and talk into the tape recorder using a bold voice, play the parts of several characters, ring a bell to turn the page and used other items in the house to make noises (usually I had to take her cue and help as she couldn't always do these and still continue reading at the same time)...the slamming of a door when someone leaves a room in the story, dishes clanging at a meal, crumpling papers up, footsteps with her dad's steel-toed boots, etc. What fun she had! Often she would giggle herself into the tape and rather than rewind and begin again, she left it in. We would all start to laugh at those parts... funny!

The idea of reading a whole book is a great one. An evening to read a story will last forever on tape.

Renee Blokzyl

Cookbooks

I have been blessed to have the cookbook my mother used and that I learned to cook with. It was given to my mother as a wedding present. Inside the front cover there is the inscription from the dear aunt who helped to raise my mother. It is an old book, with nearly all the pages torn away from the ring binder, but is so lovingly cared for that the pages have all stayed loosely in their place in the book.

The Hope Chest

My mother's little notes jotted down next to each recipe are a lovely reminder of our family favorites and of the little changes we made to the recipes over the years. She also placed handprints and little drawings between the pages, that her children had made through the years and brought to her as "love offerings" while she was in the kitchen cooking.

As I flip through the pages, I never know what little treasures will be sitting between the recipes. These treasures may not be special to others, but they are to me because they are a part of my family. I have carried on this hidden tradition with my own children, and I have already seen the difference in the size of their handprints and the advancement and talent in the drawings they have given to me. Whenever I am gifted with a "special" drawing by one of my children, I quickly write the name of the child and the date on it somewhere and stick it in my set of cookbooks. I have even been known to frame and hang these little "love" pictures in the hallway.

A friend of mine also learned to cook from the same cookbook I did, though she no longer has a copy of it. When my friend comes to visit, she often asks if she can copy some recipes down. She has such fond memories of the food and would like to pass the enjoyment on to her family. Slowly she is accumulating the recipes of her childhood and will be passing them on to her daughter.

This is a wonderful example of how food and family

recipes can become so important to our lives, and how memories are often found in the simple dishes of our youth.

I am writing a cookbook for both our children, so that the recipes have roots for them, too. I have included all the family favorites, complete with stories of my memories of where I first had that dish, or who brought it into the family, or when it was served, and so on. I included a brief profile on each cook included in the cookbook in the introduction, so our children would know more than just the names of these contributors. I also included the news from special occasions, such as Christmas 2000 and Thanksgiving 1999 in the cookbook.

I include who was with us during that celebration, and all the special foods we cooked and served. I've been doing this on the computer, in WordPerfect (now using Word) for about 10 years. I dated it at the beginning, and it's a living work. Hopefully our children won't wonder how to make a certain thing that they remember from growing up, but can't find a recipe for. My father's favorite cake recipe was never written down, and I've tried for years to duplicate it for him on his birthdays, as his Mother did for him. I'm close, but not quite 100% on it yet! (3 layer banana cake with boiled banana filling for the frosting - very old-fashioned cake).

Joan Taylor

I have been unable to find copies of my mother's cookbook for my children, so I am slowly writing by hand the recipes we use onto pretty recipe cards and placing them into recipe boxes for each child. So many of my mother's favorite recipes were kept in her mind, and when she died, all those recipes left with her. Taking a few minutes here and there, I have been able to write my children's favorite ones down. Sometimes I make a whole night of copying recipes, and the girls help me. It's a wonderful way for them to practice their penmanship, and we date each card as we finish it. I did that as a child and enjoy seeing how "old" the recipe is or how old I was when I wrote it out!

What Belongs in a Hope Chest?

When I was still a teenager, I signed up with a book company to receive one cookbook per month. I paid for these books by babysitting at church. When I had all 20 volumes I was so thrilled! This set of cookbooks contains very old recipes, dating back to the birth of our country. They came complete with historical backgrounds on many of the recipes, pictures, photos and ads from long ago. We use these books nearly every day, and my daughters are learning to cook with them. I will be purchasing complete sets of these (OOP, but still available if you look for them) for each daughter's hope chest.

What books has your daughter become attached to while she has been learning to cook? Are there family recipes she enjoys that need to be written down for her? Are there favorite recipes that Grandmother makes that your daughter would like to have? Are the recipes you use or the way you cook only kept inside your head? If so, try to put those in print even if you have to "guestimate" on the amount of ingredients.

I have a book titled The Art of Home Candy-making published in 1908 that was my grandmother's, also a little notebook in her handwriting with recipes and notes. She and my grandpa made homemade Orientals. (If you don't know what they are, they are wonderful chocolate-coated cream centers - to die for!) My mother, nor her brother nor sister took up this art, but I became interested in learning how to do it a few

few years ago and my mother dug out these old books. I also have an old hunk of marble slab used in candymaking that my grandmother used. I never got to see my grandparents make this candy but my mother has vivid memories of the sound it made when it started to "set up" and the smell of the chocolate in the house. It delights her to have her daughter recreate some of those memories of her and I guess that is really where the value lies in it for me."

Barb White

Food is an essential part of family life. With it we feed our growing families and celebrate and remember our heritage. If we lose the recipes that we have been raised on, we lose a part of our heritage. All families will grow and meld together through marriage and our environment, and the foods we feed our families will reflect that growth. But we should not lose the heritage completely, and we should not lose the recipes that have been created and handed down through so many years. In this modern era of pre-packaged foods, we are quickly replacing those wonderful time-worn treasured recipes with packaged foods that have no lasting memories of special meals or special people. Nutrition is another loss with pre-packaged foods as well. Just a few moments of your time now, while you write the recipes down, will reward your daughter and her future family with a wealth of recipes that she can use either on a daily basis or for special occasions.

What Belongs in a Hope Chest?

Inspirational books

Are there books you have read that have been of great value to you in your Christian walk? Books that have great insight and inspiration in them? Books that have carried you through rough times, or have helped you deal with a difficult problem or situation? Books you have laughed with or cried over? Books that have inspired you to reach out in areas you never thought possible before?

Out of a large number of these books, I will select a choice few to place into my daughters' hope chests. This is not because I expect them to be read right away but because there may be a time when she is searching or struggling, and these books will be readily available.

This area may seem strange to many, but I have gone through the books my mother had, and I have found tremendous help in times of trouble by reading the same ones that she went to for answers and encouragement. Often I find areas that have been marked or highlighted, and I find that sometimes I struggle with the same problems my mother did. It has been incredible to go through her books and see how she overcame different struggles. By doing this, she inadvertently left me a paper trail legacy of sorts, for which I am very thankful.

This is definitely an area that should be lifted up in prayer, and to let the Lord lead you. Books should not be given simply to fill the hope chest, but because the

The Hope Chest

Lord has touched your heart and shown you that there may be a future need that the books can help fill.

Practical Books

Practical books are teaching, reference and how-to books. Many of the titles we will be including in our daughters' hope chests are ones we have used to teach them. Others are ones that we have in the house and consider an indispensable tool for our family.

One good example is The Mary Frances Sewing Book by Jane Eayer Fryer. This is an excellent source for a child learning to sew by hand, and it's written in a sweet story form. This 1913 book has recently been re-printed and is readily available now. Throughout the story, we follow Mary Frances as she learns to sew by hand. Children can work along with Mary Frances to create a complete wardrobe for their 18 inch dolls by the end of the book. This is a wonderful book for a mother and daughter to go through together or for your daughter to learn from on her own.

Jane Eayre Fryer was a home economics teacher in the 1920's, and she wrote a total of six books for girls. Her book The Mary Frances Garden Book is also excellent for a wealth of garden knowledge. Written in a way that children can easily understand and delight in, the story line follows the garden's growth and includes all the many inhabitants of a flower or vegetable garden. This makes a wonderful read-aloud as well as a primer on gardening.

The Mary Frances Knitting and Crocheting Book, though a little more challenging for children, is also a very good source of instruction as it follows along in story form.

These simple children's books will be included in my daughters' hope chests. They can refer back to them for information and also teach their children just as they have been taught. Along with these books, which I consider to be nearly complete in themselves, I will be including other books or booklets. One very good example would be the J.P. Coats Embroidery Booklet, which has over 100 different but common embroidery stitches. A book with very basic knitting and crocheting patterns will also be included. I would consider these to be companion books to the Mary Frances books. As time goes on, and I read through various other books, I may add to or delete these companion books, but the basic idea is there to build upon.

Polly's Birth Book by Polly Block is another title my daughters will be taking with them. As a former nurse and now mother of seven children, I consider this one of the best reference books I have found on caring for the female body before, during and after pregnancy.

The Merck Manual of Medical Information: Home Edition, by Merck Research Laboratories is another very good resource that I will be including. This is a basic book covering most medical conditions. It explains the condition, gives causes if known, provides common symptoms, how it is diagnosed, the prognosis and common treatments. I would expect that some of the information would become outdated with future medical breakthroughs, but this would still be a very good resource for a new wife and future mother to have on hand.

The Encyclopedia of Country Living by Carla Emery is another choice we have made for our children's hope chests. Our family lives in the country and has a large garden area, small orchard and has raised animals for meat, milk and eggs. Our family priorities and what we want to teach our children will differ from other families. So for us this book fits our lifestyle and is a great reference on every aspect of country living.

Whenever possible we buy hardback books for their long-lasting quality and the sense of pleasure found in holding a well-made edition. What books have you found that have been a wonderful asset to you and that your daughter may find helpful one day? Have you considered whether you will spend a little extra for a hardback, or will a paperback copy do? Will you buy a new or used book? It would be wonderful for your daughter to have helpful books already on hand that she will not need to purchase at the beginning of her marriage.

Each family should consider what its priorities and lifestyles are. Families will have different needs, and their interests will vary. There is no right or wrong book to include. It all comes down to your heartfelt choices for your daughter and what will be a blessing to her. Some may feel there is no need to set aside books and will instead concentrate on other items for the hope chest.

Again, these are just some of our choices, and I am using them as an example of types of books you may want to consider including in the hope chest. Whatever is in your heart is what should be considered and not what others do for their daughters.

Historically Accurate Books

History today is being forgotten, and it is often re-written in light of our modern-day ideals, by people who have never witnessed the events. For example, how can anyone in this modern age even begin to conceive of what life was like in 1620 when the Pilgrims landed in the New World? Their near starvation, the loss of half of their number during the first winter. Their unshakable belief that God set them on their course to the New World, to be stepping stones for others who would follow behind.

How much true fact do our children know? The modern, watered-down version is what is taught today. Unless we go back and read what was written by the people who LIVED IT, we don't truly know what it was like, what they suffered, or what their beliefs were.

These first-hand accounts are becoming more and more scarce, and several generations have now been raised with the modern re-written view of what history

was... or what is more often the case what today's author either assumed was true, read from another modern writer or wants to believe based on preconceived
notions. These new books often leave out important information, or they are written with one sided, opinion-
ated worldviews that do not allow different viewpoints,
even when faced with an eyewitness account written
several hundred years ago!

But here I cannot but make a pause, and
stand half amazed at this poor people's present
condition; and so I think will the reader, too,
when he considers it well. Having thus passed the
vast ocean, and that sea of troubles before while
they were making their preparations, they now
had no friends to welcome them, nor inns to entertain and refresh their weatherbeaten bodies,
nor houses - much less towns - to repair to.

It is recorded in scripture (Acts 28) as a
mercy to the apostle and his shipwrecked crew,
that the barbarians showed them no small kindness in refreshing them; but these savage barbarians when they met with them (as will appear)
were readier to fill their sides full of arrows than
otherwise! As for the season, it was winter, and
those who have experienced the winters of this
country know them to be sharp and severe, and
subject to fierce storms, when it is dangerous to
travel to known places - much more to search an
unknown coast. Besides, what could they see but
a desolate wilderness, full of wild beasts and wild
men; and what multitude there might be of them

What Belongs in a Hope Chest?

they knew not!

———————————————

If they looked behind them, there was the mighty ocean which they had passed, and was now a gulf separating them from all civilized parts of the world. If it be said that they had their ship to turn to, it is true; but what did they hear daily from the captain and crew? That they should quickly look out for a place with their shallop, where they would be not far off; for the season was such that the captain would not approach nearer to the shore till a harbour had been discovered which he could enter safely; and that the food was being consumed apace, but he must and would keep sufficient for the return voyage. It was even muttered by some of the crew that if they did not find a place in time, they would turn them and their goods ashore and leave them.

———————————————

What then, could now sustain them but the spirit of God, and His grace? Ought not the children of their fathers rightly to say: Our fathers were Englishmen who came over the great ocean, and were ready to perish in this wilderness; but they cried unto the Lord, and He heard their voice, and looked on their adversity...Let them therefore praise the Lord, because He is good, and His mercies endure forever. Yea, let them that have been redeemed of the Lord, show how He hath delivered them from the hand of the opressor. When they wandered forth into the desert-wilderness, out of the way, and found no city to dwell in, both hungry and thirsty, their soul was overwhelmed in them. Let them confess before the Lord His loving kindness, and His wonderful works before the sons of men!

— — — — — — — — — — —

But soon a most lamentable blow fell upon them. In two or three months time half of their company died, partly owing to the severity of the winter, especially during January and February, and the want of houses and other comforts; partly to scurvy and other diseases, which their long voyage and their incommodious quarters had brought upon them. Of all the hundred odd persons, scarcely fifty remained, and sometimes two or three persons died in a day. In the time of worst distress, there were but six or seven sound persons, who, to their great commendation be it spoken, spared no pains night or day, but with great toil and at the risk of their own health, fetched wood, made fires, prepared food for the sick, made their beds, washed their infected clothes, dressed and undressed them; in a word did all the homely and necessary services for them which dainty and queasy stomachs cannot endure to hear mentioned; and all this they did willingly and cheerfully, without the least grudging, showing their love for the friends and brethren; a rare example and worthy to be remembered.

What Belongs in a Hope Chest?

Two of these seven were Mr. William Brewster, their reverend elder, and Myles Standish, their captain and military commander, to whom myself and many others were much beholden in our low and sick condition. And yet the Lord so upheld these men, that in this general calamity they were not at all infected with sickness. And what I have said of these few, I should say of many others who died in this general visitation, and others yet living, that while they had health or strength, they forsook none that had need of them. I doubt not that their recompense is with the Lord.

William Bradford, Written 1608-1650

The Hope Chest

A simple book, and yet it paints an awesomely accurate history of our Pilgrim fathers. After reading through this book, I was very humbled and thankful that God had placed the burden of starting this new country on the shoulders of these devout and godly men. Written by William Bradford, who lived through the entire experience, it shows the deep trust and faith the pilgrims had in God. This is not a politically correct book - instead, it is a truthful, fact-filled journal of who these pilgrims were and what they believed. This is a "must have" book for each of my children, and luckily it has been reprinted in a beautiful hardback version.

This is just one example of many wonderful history books that my children will have set aside for them and that they can share with their own children.

If you are drawn to collect these types of books, and to include them in your daughter's hope chest, then I have no doubt that the Lord will put them in your path.

Religious Books

This area of book collecting was brought to my attention by a mother who collects special books for her children covering all aspects of their religion. Through discussion we both realized that this is an area many families may want to consider, and for which some families may already be collecting books.

These informative can be wonderful at explaining the religious customs and the reasons behind the different celebrations, as well as giving instructions on how each of the celebrations should be carried out. These books would also be a wonderful heritage to pass on to children and grandchildren, especially if there are special ones you already have and use.

Ethnic Books

Americans are a hodgepodge of ethnicity and cultural backgrounds, all thrown together into the huge American Melting Pot. As a people, we have taken many of our country's traditions from the customs of other countries, and these traditions have been accepted into our hearts and lives.

For those who have a definite cultural heritage and would like to provide information for future generations on their culture, you may want to find books about this heritage that you enjoy and agree with, and include them in your daughter's hope chest.

Someone who has immigrated from one country to another, for example, may want to find several books that cover their homeland and also provide pictures and information on the culture, geography and history of their birth country.

This, as well as your own thoughts and memories of your homeland, or what your parents remember, could be written down in a journal for your future grandchildren. This is a wonderful personal link to a heritage that could easily be forgotten.

The Hope Chest

Personal Picture Book From Your Child

This is a fun topic. This is where you put all those adorable squiggles that your daughter made when she first held a crayon. This includes the little "thank you" notes that she made and the "get well" cards and favorite schoolwork papers. This is a memory album that you can create starting at any point in her life, adding faithfully to it with pictures, napkins from her birthday parties, pressed flowers from a special occasion, ribbons she has won; anything that can go in here should.

Even if you don't get a chance to place them all in an album, at least have a shoebox that you can place them in with a pencil handy to write her name and the date on the item. In the future, when you have time, you can sit down and work on this album. By quickly labeling the back before you store it, you don't have to worry about which daughter it belonged to or when the paper or event happened. Imagine what it would be like for her to pull that album out and leaf through it with HER children and again later when she is a grandmother and can show her grandchildren.

One mother has provided albums, stickers and special paper for her daughters to use to create their own books. These are given as birthday presents, at Christmas and during the hot summer months. During the long winter months and the hotter summer months, she and her daughters work on the books together. Her daughters are not only learning how to create scrap-books themselves, and making memories in the process, but they are enjoying the time they share and work to-gether on the project. By the time they are grown, each daughter will have several albums that hold memories, pictures and bits of her life within their pages. This would be a fun tradition to start!

A little effort now can bring many wonderful memories for your daughter, as well as grandchildren and great-grandchildren who are still only a vague and distant thought in your mind...faceless little ones who will one day giggle and with a chubby finger trace over the lines that your own dearest daughter drew with her tiny hands when she was young.

Family Pictures & History Scrapbook

This is an area so often overlooked. Can you think back and remember the family stories that your parents and grandparents told to you as a child? Who was who, and who married who? What was the name of your mother's best friend when she was a child? What was the name of your father's dog when he was a little boy? Where did they grow up? What was your grand-mother's favorite recipe? What did your grandfather do for a living? How did your grandparents meet and what happened at their wedding? How did your parents meet and why did they give you the name they did? Were there any important things in the family background that should not be forgotten? Heroic deeds, family moves, artistic or music talent, any inventors or historic people in the family archives? What were the professions of your ancestors, and what were their homes like? So many questions and many that your children and grandchildren will ask you.

If you don't take the time to write it down now, it can easily be lost forever. Children are always curious about their family and what has happened in the past. Make the effort to provide this for your grandchildren while your children are still young. Turn it into a family project if you need help, with grandparents and your own siblings helping to put together a scrapbook of memories, photos and other important events and family history. Try putting it together in black and white, and offer to provide copies to everyone in the family who helps put it together. Make it a fun time, maybe meeting once or twice a year for just one afternoon and doing as much as you can. This could easily be turned into a fun family tradition that will be a wonderful gift for future children!

Another very good way to record the family history, memories and special stories is to make a taped recording of the grandparents or great-grandparents as they tell the stories to your children. Family get-togethers are also a good time to pull out the recorder and sit around "talking" about these things. It may not be a well-edited or pretty copy, but it will be a realistic one with the voices, verbal inflections and accents of the people involved. And what a wonderful gift to your daughter, her husband and future grandchildren to hear your daughter's voice as a child! MAKE the time!

> If you have a grandparent or great-grandparent alive...run, don't walk...with a tape recorder or video camera...anything to preserve them for future reflections. My husband took our video camera and taped Grandmother, and I enjoy looking through them. All her memories and details of the folks in these albums (old black and white photos) are what we used after she died to rebuild our heritage albums up complete with all the journaling she spoke of in her sweet ramblings. Their voices will send *love chills* up and down your spine as you remember them fondly with love, listening to them speak."

Renee Blokzyl

My mom was good about doing this with my grandparents so we have some wonderful tapes with stories on them. She was sure to take the tape recorder to family reunions also and informally interviewed her aunts and uncles.

When I left home for college, my Mom would leave the tape recorder running during meal times and send the tapes to me. Later, after I'd married, my grandparents moved in with my parents. My grandfather had Alzheimer's andoften my mom would leave the tape recorder running during meal times. She captured some funny conversations with him.

The Hope Chest

My Mom and I exchanged audio tapes for years after I'd married and moved 1000 miles away, and while I taped over many of these, we still have many of them also. I wish now I'd not taped over ANY of them!

Dawn

Another idea, is to make copies of all the old family photos, and put those into a photo album with as much information as you can under each picture. With today's modern printers and the photo paper available at most stores, this is easily done and often the reprints look as authentic as the originals.

My mother-in-law has many old family pictures with faded names on the back of a very select few and no other information. It is a guessing game of who is who and where they all belong in the family. Why the picture was taken, what was going on in the picture and what year it was taken is an endless mystery. With a little forethought, and with the help of older or elderly relatives, quite a bit of that history can be put down and recorded. But it needs to be done before those old "walking family history books" are gone and their memories forever silenced.

Even if you work with the pictures and the family scrapbook only one day out of the whole year trying to unravel the puzzle, it will be well worth the effort down the road, and your grandchildren will have a legacy of their family history in pictures and written memories.

What Belongs in a Hope Chest?

If your parents and in-laws have all these pictures, ask if they would do this project for your daughter's hope chest. If they are unable to, ask to borrow the pictures, and maybe they would be willing to help supply you with the information while you compile the album. Often the only other alternative for these pictures is to divide them between family members. Within a generation or two these pictures are so spread out that they become meaningless and are often discarded because no one knows the history or cares enough to find out. The family history vanishes along with the pictures. With a little care now, the family history can easily be spared.

With today's photo-quality printers and photo paper, there really is no excuse for not having an album for each child. All it takes is a few minutes here and there, and those moments can add up to a wonderful treasure hidden in the depths of the hope chest.

Another very good way to preserve old family photos is to have them professionally mounted and framed. Although this is more expensive, it provides long-term use and protection of the photo. Professional mounting allows nice photographs to be displayed to their best advantage, and can it be a wonderful idea, especially when it resembles someone in the present-day family.

Our daughter looks just like my husband's grandmother, who died decades before my husband was born. For Christmas, we copied the one photograph we have of her and framed it for our daughter's main Christmas gift. She was thrilled with that heirloom, because she so resembles this unknown grandmother. We only know that this lady loved the Lord, and asked her only son, my husband's father, to become a pastor, which he later did. My father-in-law was 5 when his mother died.

Joan Taylor

Family genealogy has made a big comeback, and it is much easier now to find out about your family's lineage. There are many different computer programs that will help you search on the internet and help find information for you, with very little effort on your part.

Family history was a legacy handed down through a written account found in the family Bible, or through the memories of parents, grandparents and great-grandparents. This information can be so easily lost through time, the loss of a family Bible, and the deaths of loved ones.

My mother was taught from a very young age all the family history on her father's side of the family. This included the names, birthdates, historical battles the men fought in from the Revolutionary War to the Korean War, where the family lived and moved, the historical memory of the wagon trip from Illinois to Nevada, even the hair color and eye color of many family members going as far back as the Revolutionary War. Unfortunately my mother never wrote any of this down, and when she died I was left with only scattered information that she had told me about when I was young.

Trying to rebuild this information is very slow going. The struggle for information has made such a big impression on me, how a few minutes of writing down information could have saved so much research and expense later on. But as a child I never even considered this aspect of life, and my mother no doubt felt she had plenty of time to write it down at some future point.

It has been rewarding, though, to find the names and information about my ancestors. Many names that I am partial to were actually family names. It would have been fun to know all about my family history before I had children, as I may have used many of those old names for my own children, and I could have passed on a legacy through names.

It was once customary to place the bride's lineage on a large piece of parchment paper and place this in her hope chest. The groom would fill in his side when the betrothal agreement was finalized. How easy it would be to revive this little custom. As one mother suggested, take a parchment with the family tree on it, and fill in your daughter's side, then place it inside the lid of the hope chest for safe-keeping. When your daughter becomes engaged, it is a simple matter to take it out and fill in as much information as possible on the groom's side and place it back inside the lid again. This keeps it wrinkle free, and each time the lid is opened it shows the lineage of the married couple.

> I think it would be good to have a family tree that was in two halves. My daughter has filled out her half and when she is engaged she could give the other half to her fiancée and he could fill it out. When they are married they can put it in the top of the hope chest together... Pam True

Recipes

I have a small wooden recipe box that holds treasures: the recipes that I collected as a child and teenager, the few recipes my mother copied by hand for me, cut-out recipes from the backs of boxes and the labels of cans...a large assortment of this and that. These are treasures that are often irreplaceable.

Have you ever lost a favorite recipe and looked everywhere for it, becoming more and more disappointed and upset because it was lost and gone forever? Imagine your daughter married and moving away or even losing you. The recipes that she grew up with, the smells of the foods she loved and watched you cook, the family favorites that she wants to prepare but can't remember how. This can easily be prevented by a simple recipe box, some index cards, and the time you and your daughter take to copy the recipes from your file to hers.

I say this from experience. When my mother died, the recipes that were not written down were lost with her. I made up my own variations through the years, and I was blessed with a few lists of ingredients that she had hastily written down on scraps of paper and tossed into her old cookbook. But I lost many of my favorite ones because they were kept in my mother's "mental recipe file" and had never been written down.

If you and your relatives can find the time to get together and put these family heirlooms on paper, your daughter can enjoy them and pass them on to future generations. Make a party out of it, or have a "favorite family recipe" contest. The winner could be given a new recipe box! Create memories while getting the work done. Our forefathers and mothers knew the importance of this. Corn huskings, quilting bee's and barn raisings are only a few examples of finding a fun way to make the work go faster.

When your daughter becomes engaged, throw a recipe party for both sides of the family. Encourage the groom's mother and relatives to help fill the recipe box with recipes he has enjoyed growing up or that are a tradition in his family. This is a very special and easy way to get to know your in-laws. You might like to have all these special recipes placed on recipe cards that are a certain color, or that have a special look, layout or illustration on them, especially if they will be going into a recipe box. This will help them stand out against the multitude of other wonderful recipes. Of course, if at all possible, have them hand-written.

A nice offering for the bride during this party would

be to give her a book that holds recipe cards. Each card would slide into place during the party, and the person giving the recipe could explain why they chose that particular recipe. If possible, someone should volunteer to write the information down, so it can be included in the book when all the recipes have been given to the bride.

We have a rubber stamp set that we use on card stock to make some of our own recipe cards. We also pick up the pretty printed ones that we find on sale occasionally. Once the recipe has been written out, we slip a laminating sheet over it and slide it through the laminator. This helps protects the recipe card for the long term and is relatively inexpensive. Our laminator was an investment that has paid off in many unforeseen ways, including the recipe cards. I have also been able to laminate the pages of my mother's old cookbook so they are no longer flaking off in dried paper flakes. The pages fit neatly into a three-ring binder now. Laminators can be purchased at most office supply stores. I would recommend a heat laminator as opposed to a cold one as it does a much better job.

My daughters practice their handwriting skills by copying the recipes, and they are slowly accumulating a legacy of family favorites. Each daughter has a recipe box that she stained or painted herself, and the cards go inside, waiting to be used one day in her future home. Decoupage is a fun way to decorate a recipe box, whether it's wood, plastic or metal.

What Belongs in a Hope Chest?

When you are making copies of recipes, don't forget to include any favorite recipes that other family members, friends or church families may have. Those church pot-luck meals often provide some of the tastiest foods we have ever eaten! Track down the recipes of the ones that you or your daughter really enjoyed. The recipe owner will no doubt be pleased by your interest, and it may bless her to know you are asking for her recipe to include in your daughter's hope chest.

As well as favorite recipes, try to make sure that the basic recipes are also included. Basic cake, cookie, biscuit, bread and pie crust recipes are essential. Cooking times for a turkey or ham and suggestions for what herb to use with what kind of meat are useful. Substitutions for common ingredients if she runs out can be very handy too, as well as conversions in measurement. On a single recipe card you can place how many teaspoons make a tablespoon, how many tablespoons in a quarter cup, etc. Pulling out a card with the information on it is often easier and quicker than looking it up in a large cookbook.

What about mixes? Are there any special family mixes that should be written down? There is a family we know who enjoys mixing three kinds of pepper together and rubbing it on their meat prior to barbecuing it. Another family makes a wonderful chicken marinade from honey, orange juice and curry powder. Treasures like this should be placed onto recipe cards before they are overlooked or forgotten. Your future grandchildren will be thankful you did!

The ultimate goal of the recipe box is to help your daughter. Newly married and trying to please her husband, she will have so many wonderful meals to choose from at her fingertips! That old saying, "The way to a man's heart is through his stomach" is not that far off. A husband who enjoys his wife's cooking and looks forward to coming home to a home-cooked meal will be a blessing to his wife, and she will find joy in pleasing him.

Linens and Household Items

Linens were a common item found in nearly every hope chest in by-gone eras. Each piece of clothing as well as every linen in the house, whether bed sheets or kitchen towels, had to be made by hand for the family's use. Sometimes the fabric was made on small table looms by the family members themselves and then turned into useful items instead of purchasing the cloth. Fabric, linen, any type of cloth was a valuable asset and a time-consuming item to attain. Great care was taken not only in making the item but in purchasing or hiring someone to create specific items. Linen, fabric and cloth were items laundered and cared for properly for the longest use possible.

Today we have the ease and comfort of readily available sheets, towels and all other necessary items.

What Belongs in a Hope Chest?

However, these items have replaced needle skills that were taught, practiced and prized through generations of women. Modern children are being raised without ever learning the basics of needle handiwork, let alone the beauty of the advanced skills. Instead of the elegance of hand-embroidered bed sheets, pillowcases, tablecloths and table runners, and all the other linens that were worked on and cherished, we have become a society where heirloom quality is so easily replaced by materialistic factory-produced items. What seems so strange is that anything labeled "handmade" by the lady of the house is thought to be somewhat lower in standard compared to store-bought items. But when we find a "handmade" item in a store, it has a high price tag attached. This is a puzzle that has never been explained to me.

The mass-produced items do have their place in our homes, but we should not relinquish the past skills completely. By taking the time and effort to make beautiful articles for our homes, whether for a daughter's future home or the one we are raising our children in now, we show a special love for each person through our hands. Home reflects the heart of the wife and mother. If we spend the time and effort to make heirloom items that are well cared for and sent along with our children to their future homes, we are sending a part of our heart and our love with them as well.

The beauty that surrounds our family is no less important than the material items we can provide for them. Purchasing very inexpensive embroidery flosses and needles, or other embellishments for the linens we use, and taking the time to make the ordinary become beautiful, we show that our family is very dear to us and worth the effort.

This does not need to be hard or expensive! There are so many simple and easy ways to turn ordinary items into beautiful treasures. Fabric and craft stores are full of ideas. Booklets give detailed instructions, material lists and photos as well. Creativity is God-given, it is an extension of Himself that He has given to man. With a little effort, anyone can create little items and slowly expand to larger, more detailed items.

This section will cover more than just linens, and you should not be limited to fabric items only. Look around you at what is in your home, what you use on a daily or weekly basis and how you can make these ordinary items more beautiful. Have your children help you come up with ideas too, and teach them how the everyday simple things can be creatively decorated for a more pleasing look.

Crocheted or tatted lace can be added around the edge of linens, or store-bought lace can be used. If embroidery is not an option for you, there are tube paints and fabric ink pens that can be substituted, or any number of other products can be used. Although embroidery or needlepoint is the most common and traditional method of decorating linens, there are other options for decoration as well. Your fabric or craft store is the best place to start.

You will find many ideas through catalogs that specialize in sewing and handiwork and many are listed in the appendix. Try what appeals to you and your daughter. Many of the age-old arts are slowly being lost through non-use and through the deaths of the older generations who were raised knowing them. Very few people today have taken the time and effort to learn these old skills, and very few have been passed onto the new generations. Within a short period of time, some of these skills may become extinct and will only be seen on old linens in museums.

By teaching your daughter some of these skills, you not only help to bring enjoyment through the hands to the mind, but you may allow your daughter to use those skills later to earn a small income at home if she is ever in need.

Here are a few examples of handiwork arts that are quickly disappearing and becoming legend: tatting, embroidery, crewel, needlepoint, tapestry, crocheted lace, knitted lace, ribbon embroidery, hardanger, cross stitch, appliqué, French or heirloom sewing and smocking, to name only a few.

If you are not able to learn these skills, beautiful items can still be made very simply. Just by sewing on lace that has ribbon threaded through it can perk up a drab pillowcase or bath towel, and the ribbon adds to the color scheme of the room. Crocheting a lacy edge directly along the edge of the pillowcase or sheet, instead of sewing on store-bought lace, can also make it look nicer and last longer. Ribbons and lace applied to any item have the ability to soften a room and give a warm, homey welcome to family and friend alike. These are only a few ideas; you and your daughter can find many many more.

When you are making items for the hope chest, it is better to use the same design pattern for each complete set of linens, towels, kitchen accessories, etc. If there are several different designs that your daughter wishes to use, then each complete set of linens should have the same design used for each separate set. This makes it easier to match later when she is changing sheets, towels and other items, and it allows a nice change so she does not become bored with the same pattern for years.

Traditionally, monogramming initials should always be of the same design, so care should be taken in choosing the letter style. There are countless monogram initials you can use. One of the simplest and easiest ways to find a good monogramming initial is to use a font on your computer. Choose a letter font that is pleasing to you, one that can be used easily for either embroidery, fabric ink pens or tube paints. You can make larger or smaller monogrammed initials simply by increasing or decreasing the size going through the printer or copy machine. It may be a good idea to have several different sizes on one piece of paper so you can choose which size of monogramming looks more proportioned to the item on which you are working. Keep the paper for future use by folding and placing it inside your daughter's sewing basket. One sheet with several different sizes can be re-used countless times when you are using the window highlighting technique. The same idea can be used for any design you choose for linens; make several different sizes and keep the original for future use.

The window highlighting technique is fairly simple. During daytime hours when there is ample sunlight, tape your monogram pattern to a window pane. Tape your fabric over the monogram pattern, centering the pattern on the fabric. Trace with a pencil. You have now transferred your pattern to your fabric and are ready for sewing.

If you would like to add a monogram to towels, it would be a good idea to first embroider the monogram onto a nice piece of linen or fabric, and then appliqué that directly onto the towel. A circular or oval piece of fabric would be the best to use and would allow a nice, even hem when appliquéd to the towel. Add a little more embellishment if you like with lace or ribbon. There is no easy way to transfer patterns onto terry towel fabric. The only other option is to have the towels monogrammed by a store that has the right equipment. This can be pricey however, especially if you would like the whole set monogrammed. You can, however, make thick flannel hand towels to match the color of the terry towels, and transfer the monogram initial directly to the flannel. Flannel towels absorb much better than terry towels made from polyester/ cotton blends, are softer, and can be easily replaced with newly made ones when the old ones wear out. This may allow you to have the larger terry towels monogrammed through a store, while you do the smaller hand towels yourself and save a little money.

Linen Items

Let's start with the traditional linen items first. What kind of linens would you and your daughter like to place in her hope chest? Make a list, and keep it handy to add more items when you think of them. Here are a few of the more common items found in the older hope chests and how you can make them simply and inexpensively.

Pillowcases

Pillowcases are very easy. These can be bought pre-stamped from a wide variety of stores or catalogs. You can also easily make your own designs, or add your own monogramming to plain pillowcases that you have purchased straight from the store shelves. If you would like to use iron-on transfers, there are a number of those available, or you can simply trace the pattern of your choice onto the edge of the pillowcase and embroider. Using your computer to make monogrammed initials or any text you would like, and using computer pictures or click-art printed onto paper, can provide you with a wide variety of patterns for the pillowcases without ever leaving your home.

If you do not have computer access, using pictures from books, coloring books, hand-drawn pictures or other areas, allows you to trace a large number of patterns or designs onto the pillowcase edge to embroider. This may take a little more time if you need to trace a copy from the book onto paper, and then use the paper copy to place in the window or a light box and trace onto fabric, but it is easily done and very inexpensive.

When you have the same matching design on the pillowcase edges and the top edge of the top sheet, you have a nice matching set of bed linens. Simply adding dresser scarves or runners, with the same design and thread color, creates a beautiful matching bedroom set for your daughter's hope chest.

Sheets

Long ago, great care was taken with the embroidery sewn along the top edge of the top sheet, especially the bed linens destined for the hope chest. These were special linens that were to start the couple off on their new life together, and the sheets were often made from very strong cloth that would last through years and years of use. It was considered an investment for the future to have the best possible linen, and parents would purchase the very best they could afford.

The Hope Chest

Today there is no need to make the actual sheets. Instead sheet sets can be bought and the edges embroidered or otherwise decorated. The size of the sheets may be your biggest decision. Full-size or queen-size is often the best choice, leaning more towards the queen size. A queen-sized top sheet can still fit onto a full-sized bed with extra length hanging over the sides, but a full-sized top sheet may not be wide enough if placed onto a queen-size bed. The same for the bottom sheet. Most couples today start off with a queen-size bed and later they often move to a king-sized bed. The original sheets from your daughter's hope chest can then be used for a daughter's bed or a guest room, or tucked back into the hope chest for future use.

Plan ahead to purchase sheets and bedding items and look for store sales or close-outs. Local stores and mail order catalogs often have wonderful sales with substantial savings at the end of the season. If you plan carefully and set aside a little money for these sales, you can purchase very good quality sheets. Often the prices fall to half or more off the regular sale price. Look for high thread counts and try to make sure the sheets and pillowcases match even if they are plain white. The fabric should be of the same quality and texture. If you are unsure of what to look for, go by thread count. The bottom line you should consider is 200 thread count sheets. With thread counts of 220 you will find your average percale sheets. Sheets with a 250 thread count are usually Supima cotton or high quality percale. 320 thread count sheets are usually Supima cotton or sateen. At 400 thread count you find sateen, petite jardin and pinpoint oxford. Above 400 you will find egyptian cotton, linen and other very high quality threads and blended threads. The higher the thread count, the more costly the linen. The price will pay off in the end however. Low thread counts will wear out quicker and become coarse with washing.

If at all possible, white top sheets should be used, or cream or ecru if white is not appealing to your daughter. The embellished top sheet can easily be matched with a new bottom sheet if a different size is needed or the bottom sheet wears out. If your daughter wishes to add more color by having a solid colored bottom sheet, the original white top sheet can still be used. Top sheets usually outlast bottom sheets, and with a white top sheet the ability to prolong its use by matching worn out bottom sheets has an advantage. Frugality walks hand in hand with elegance here.

When decorating the top edge of the sheet, there will need to be a decision on where to place the design. Will you have the design on both top corners and along the direct center, or will it be placed across the entire length of the top sheet edge? Both are appropriate, it is only personal choice that is the deciding factor. When you have decided where you will place the design, the next step is to find a design you like. You will need to make it proportional to the edge of the sheet. If the design is too small, you will need to enlarge it on a copy

machine. If the design is too large, shrink it to size.
Once you have transferred the image onto the fabric, it
simply needs to be embroidered, painted with fabric
paints, colored with fabric pens, have ribbon embroidery applied or finished with whichever method of
decoration you choose.

The design on the pillowcases, bureau runners or
scarves are all done in the same manner you used with
the sheet. Make sure the design matches whatever linens will be used, and make the pattern proportional to
the size of the item you will be making. Obviously with
a small linen item, you will need to shrink the pattern
in size, which will allow the item to look balanced. This
can be done in a copy store or using your own scanner
and printer. Use your own good judgment to choose the
appropriate size you need. If in doubt, make several different sizes and tape onto your window. Then place the
item to be decorated over each sized pattern, and you
will see which looks best.

There is the option of adding lace to enhance the
set, both along the top sheet edge and the pillowcase
edges. Today there are many cotton laces available that
look as if they are hand crocheted or have been tatted
by hand, and these wash very well. If you would like to
dye the cotton lace to match the embroidery or a colored bottom sheet, make sure you choose a dye that is
colorfast once it sets or use a product that helps hold in
the dye. You can also thread slender colored ribbons
through the white cotton lace to match the color

scheme of the room, and if the room colors ever change, you can simply replace the ribbon. With the addition of matching lace around the edge to highlight the linen's decoration, you have a beautiful set for the new little home.

If all this sounds too hard to accomplish, remember it is simply a small step away from the pre-stamped sets that can be purchased. By taking the extra steps of choosing a special design that your daughter enjoys, sizing the pattern and tracing it onto the linens, you will be able to create a very special and personal linen set.

Dresser Scarves, Table Runners & Doilies

These are easy to make and really add beauty to any room, as well as covering scratched surfaces on used furniture which many newly married couples start off with. By using 100% cotton muslin, either the plain natural color or bleached white muslin, you have an inexpensive fabric that can be used to make any kind of household linen.

To make the dresser scarves, measure the piece of furniture it will be placed on. Measure from where you would like one side of the dresser scarf to start, and where the other side will end. Cut the fabric according to the length you choose, making sure you leave enough for a seam or hem allowance. If you wish to curve each end, fold in half lengthwise and use a plate or other round object to trace the curve from. If you would like to have edges with a specific design, such as a point or long scallops along the edge, or with a certain angle to it, make a pattern on paper. Work with the pattern until it is just what you want, then trace it onto the fabric and cut the fabric accordingly.

The edges should be hemmed to prevent the fabric from fraying as you work on it. You can hem the edges several different ways. One way is turning the edges under, and working a running stitch along the top edge by hand or machine. Or the edge can be rolled under if you crochet a lace border around the item. You can also use a satin stitch, whip stitch or blanket stitch around the edge. You can use a sewing machine for these stitches, or if you are sewing by hand, use embroidery floss for a simple decoration. Even plain white embroidery floss makes your items look more elegant than plain thread. If you use three strands of floss instead of six, it will have a thinner, flatter finish to it. Using 6 strands will elevate the edge slightly for a different look. If you are using a sewing machine or serger, and would like to make the edges look special, try using gold, silver or colored metallic threads. I have even seen a pearlized colored thread that picks up surrounding colors, which would be very nice to place around the edges of a runner or dresser scarf.

Once the fabric is cut to the size you need, and the edges have been hemmed, trace the desired design onto the fabric and embroider or decorate however you wish. Hand wash or wash on the gentle cycle in the washing machine, dry and iron before carefully placing inside the hope chest. If the item needs to be folded, use tissue paper between the creases to help prevent any wrinkles or folds that will hard to iron out later.

Table runners are done the same way, only they are usually longer than a dresser scarf. The design on the table runners traditionally have some kind of fruit, vegetable or cornucopia on it if food will be served on the table. But of course anything can be used and in any color scheme your daughter would like.

For tables that are not used for food, such as hallway tables or coffee tables, the designs on these linens usually have a flower, leaf or line design on them. This is the traditional way, but any design that you and your daughter enjoy should and can be used. This is what creates unique and special linens for your daughter's hope chest. Give hardanger or pulled thread needlework a try. It is very similar to cross stitch and very easy to learn. Hardanger, either alone or with embroidery, lends a very beautiful "old world" charm to any item.

Doilies are fairly easy to crochet, and patterns are easily found in all craft and fabric stores. If you are not able to make doilies and would like to find some handmade ones to include in the chest, there are many places to start looking for them. Estate sales, garage sales, thrift stores, flea markets, auctions, antique stores, boutique stores, newspaper ads, eBay, and if all else fails, try placing an ad in a fabric store, craft store, or or newspaper looking for someone who will make them for you for a fee.

Kitchen Towels & Dishcloths

There are many factory-made kitchen towels that are pretty as well as useful. This is one area that mothers and daughters may wish to skip; however, hand-embroidered kitchen towels are very beautiful and add a simple elegance to the kitchen.

Flour sack towels or muslin towels last much longer than the loose-weave terry cloth towels so consider this area carefully before skipping by. A set of a dozen white flour sack dish towels, or 100% cotton muslin towels, would be enough for a new bride's kitchen. For sparkling glasses and silverware, a linen towel is best, although flannel towels are also a good choice. Both can be either bought or handmade. A stiff polishing from these towels helps put a sparkling shine on most glassware and takes the spots off of silverware.

Probably you will number among your wedding gifts some beautiful pieces of glass, which will require care to keep them clear and sparkling.

The easiest and best way to clean glassware, especially the beautiful clear crystal, whose real beauty far surpasses the much-cut kind so popular a few years ago, is to wash it in warm water in pure soap. Rinse in warm water and dry with a clean, lint less towel. If the glass be greasy, as a glass that held milk or a glass bowl filled with ice cream, it should be rinsed in cold water before washing.

If your cut glass needs a thorough washing, try this method: Wash in warm soapy water, brushing all the crevices with a soft brush, rinse, and lay in a bed of sawdust to dry. This brushing will remove every bit of soil from the deep cuts. Should you not have sawdust, give it a thorough rubbing with soft crepe paper. Vigorous friction will enhance the beauty of the glass.

The Hope Chest: A Book for the Bride, 1922

To make kitchen towels, you can easily buy "flour sack" towels from many department, discount or restaurant supply stores. These towels are 100% cotton and made from the same fabric that flour sacks are made of, only they are pure white with no decoration or print on them. These are usually inexpensive, though you may wish to shop around and find the best price. Muslin towels are made from 100% cotton muslin cloth, either natural color or white, and can be found at any fabric store. The muslin can be cut to the size desired and hemmed to create the towels. These would be even less costly than the flour sack towels. Some fabric stores actually sell what they call "toweling" material, which is a large weave fabric and also makes nice towels. These wear out faster however, since the weave is loose and more apt to rub or snag.

Any of these would be fine for embroidery or other means of decoration, though the toweling fabric may not take the tube paints well, and it may be hard to trace any design due to their thickness. All of these towels wash easily, and once they have been washed a few times are wonderful for absorbing water from wet hands and dishes. Just make sure you purchase 100% cotton as the mixed blends (polyester/cotton) do not absorb well and your daughter will be very disappointed with them.

The towels should be hemmed before you start to help prevent the fabric from fraying. When placing the design on the towel, it is usually best to center it along the bottom edge if you will be folding the towel in thirds to hang. Some may prefer to use the design on only half of the towel, thinking to fold the towel in half and hang. Decide which way you will be folding the towel and place your design appropriately.

Dish cloths are SO easily made by crocheting or knitting that there is no reason why anyone would ever need to purchase any. There are many beautiful patterns to choose from, found at most stores that sell yarn, so it is easy to choose several inexpensive booklets and create a myriad of dishcloths. If you would rather use the regular single or double crochet design, there is no need to purchase any booklets at all. Dishcloths should made using only 100% cotton yarn to allow the water to easily absorb into the fabric. Acrylic blends do not work well and are often harsh on the hands. Acrylic yarns have a tendency to stretch easily too, especially when wet. Cotton yarn can be bought in bulk skeins which will lower the cost of the final product, and there are many colors to choose from in cotton yarns. These dishcloths wash and wear very well and outlast the store-bought thinner ones.

One of my daughters, when she was seven years old, made a crocheted dishcloth to enter into a local fair. She had been crocheting for only a few months, and the pattern was a simple granny square with white in the middle and ringed with a border of deep red. When she finished her dishcloth, no one could tell whether she or her mother had made it, it was done so well. These are easy to do, and simple ones can be made in only an hour or so. They are wonderful practice for children and mothers alike who are just learning to crochet, and any extras can be given away as gifts to family and friends. These are portable projects that you can slip into a purse or backpack to work on while you are waiting in an office, at music lessons, ball games, long car rides or wherever you find a few moments of extra time.

If you will be making kitchen towels and dishcloths, keep the color theme the same so the whole set looks matched and beautiful. Whatever color is used on the kitchen towels can be reflected in the color of the cotton yarn in the dishcloths.

The Hope Chest

Kitchen Accessories

There are many wonderful patterns for hot pads, oven mitts, appliance covers and aprons. These are usually simple, easy-to-sew items that are wonderful projects for a daughter to make when she is learning to sew on a machine. One set, with extra hot pads and oven mitts, will be all your daughter should need for her hope chest. If she keeps the pattern for these items in her hope chest once she has made a set, she will have the ability to make more anytime she may need them, and the same pattern will match the items she is still using.

Aprons

These may seem to be an old-fashioned item; and they are rarely seen in any kitchen anymore, but for those women who use them, we know just how useful they really are! Aprons originally were used to keep the clothing beneath the apron clean and from being damaged by snags or stains. An apron would be donned for the daily house and kitchen work, and when unexpected company was knocking at the door the apron would suddenly be whisked away allowing the lady of the house to present a clean and ready appearance for her guests.

What Belongs in a Hope Chest?

Children were sent out to play in pinafores to protect their clothing and prolong its use. I can attest to the fact that when my own daughters wore their little aprons and pinafores over their dresses, I had fewer stains to deal with and tears to mend.

Today we have strayed from the usefulness of aprons. Although we don't need to worry about our appearance as much when guests arrive today, there are so many wonderful reasons for bringing the apron back into our homes, one of which is that special feminine feeling that comes over you the moment you don the apron! You find yourself standing a little taller and being more enthusiastic about cleaning your home, just from a little extra fabric that ties or buttons behind you.

In the kitchen, the apron is wonderful for catching those hot grease splatters and keeping them from ruining your favorite dress or blouse. It is extremely handy to dry wet hands on if a towel is not easily accessible. It also keeps your clothes cleaner, especially when using flour. For housework it is very handy if you have an apron with large deep pockets, or several pockets across the whole front of it. It can easily hold a large number of items that need to be put away in other rooms, freeing your hands from carrying them and making several trips. Laundry can be easily transported with the apron used as a carrier of sorts and holding up the corners. There are endless uses for the apron in the home.

The Hope Chest

Besides the kitchen, aprons have their use in many other areas of the home. Garden aprons, canning aprons, baby bathing aprons (use terry cloth, and wrap up baby in your apron to snuggle dry instead of in a towel), hair cutting aprons (vinyl or plastic tablecloth fabric), painting aprons, sewing aprons (lots of little pockets with a sewn-in pincushion) and many other kinds can be tailor-made to fit your projects. Aprons can be made out of any kind of fabric and can be plain or decorated.

What Belongs in a Hope Chest?

Tablecloths and Cloth Napkins

There are many kinds of tablecloths and many ways of embellishing or decorating them. There are the common vinyl-covered and flannel backed ones you can find at most stores, fancy lacy dining room tablecloths, hand-crocheted imported tablecloths and many more.

Whether you choose to make a tablecloth from loose-weave checked gingham fabric, plain white muslin or another type of fabric, size needs to be taken into account. It would be best to use a rectangular pattern and avoid the oval or circular shapes when making a tablecloth. This is because there is no way of knowing what shape table your daughter will have when she starts her new home. A rectangle shape will cover any table completely whereas a circular or oval tablecloth will show the table corners on a rectangular table.

An assortment of sizes should be made and placed into the hope chest, smaller ones to fit a card table, medium-sized and large, as well. When your daughter first marries and begins using them, there will only be two people, so the table will most likely be small. As her family grows so will the tabletop. She should also have at least one large tablecloth to use for family get-togethers, church groups or parties.

There are many types of fabric that can be used for a tablecloth and many ways to embellish it. There is the thin, colorful gingham fabric we all know so well. Muslin, calico and even taffeta can be used. Monk's cloth is nice for a thicker tablecloth. The choices are all up to you and your daughter. Other than the gingham for informal use, your daughter should have at least one very nice plain white tablecloth for special occasions. If she desires to use calicos or solid colors, care and advice should be given in picking out the color. What she likes and what may be popular now could be very different in years to come. Solid, plain colors that are either lightly or lavishly decorated would do much better in the long run than several of the current popular colors.

The ways are numerous for embellishing the tablecloth. Besides the usual embroidery, there is also cross stitch or hardanger, inserting lace along the middle, appliqué, fabric paints, a tie-dyed look, quilted borders, crocheted edges, sewn-on ribbon lengths and many other wonderful ideas.

Most tablecloths are simply hemmed with nothing special added. If you or your daughter would like to sew lace to the edge, it can add beauty to the finished product as well. Try to find lace that is made of the same kind of thread as the tablecloth for more uniformity. If the tablecloth is all cotton, try to find all-cotton lace or eyelet. If the fabric is nylon or polyester or a blend, try to find lace that will match in texture. Also choose the size of the lace that looks best with the fabric. Lace that is very short on a large tablecloth may look a little odd, and wide lace that is gathered tightly would look out of place on a small tablecloth. These simple little steps can be the difference between an eye-pleasing end result and an eye-sore that is never taken from the hope chest and used.

Napkins should be made with the same fabric as the tablecloths. If you would like lace around the edges, use short lace so the napkin will retain its proportional look. Nothing wide or tightly gathered should be used. Any design that you have used on the tablecloth can also be applied and sewn onto the napkins. If time does not permit this, leaving the napkins plain is acceptable as long as the same fabric is used for both tablecloth and napkin.

There is one way to embellish a plain white tablecloth and be able to change colors later if your daughter decides she would rather have blue instead of yellow or some other color. Cut and hem the tablecloth and napkins. Along the center of the tablecloth, or both long edges, carefully sew a length of flat or eyelet lace that allows you to thread ribbon through it. The colored ribbon your daughter chooses can be threaded through, and in the future if she decides to change the color, it is a simple thing to undo the ribbon and re-thread a new color through the lace. This allows the same tablecloth to be used with a variety of colors and for different holidays throughout the year. If your daughter wishes, she can also place the flat lace and ribbon kitty-corner across one corner of the napkins. Making several different sizes of tablecloths, and having matching napkins, both for everyday use and special occasions, allows your daughter to have a wonderful start for her new kitchen and dining room. The added embellishment, if any is used, will only enhance the effect.

Miscellaneous Linens

Afghans and Throw Blankets

Afghans are a wonderful way for you and your daughter to learn and practice crocheting and knitting. Afghans are warm and snug and easy to make. There are as many patterns to choose from as there are quilt patterns and designs, so the choices are never-ending. The types of yarn available make crocheting or knitting even more fun and exciting, and it is a wonderful project to curl up with on a cold winter's night.

When you are finished with an afghan or throw blanket, remember to wash it and dry it according to the directions on the yarn package, and then place the afghan inside a linen bag before putting in the hope chest. Even though the sides of the hope chest may be very smooth and would not snag the afghan, items inside the chest may cause snagging and could potentially ruin all your hard work. Take a few minutes to carefully pack the afghan so it will be as beautiful when your daughter takes it out to use as it was when it was placed inside the hope chest.

What Belongs in a Hope Chest?

If you are unable to make an afghan and would like to include one, there are numerous places to look for new or used ones. Thrift stores, flea markets and estate or garage sales usually offer the best possibilities. You may also be able to place an ad in newspapers, store fronts, or in a church bulletin looking for someone whom you can hire to do the work for you.

If you buy a used afghan, or any other yarn item, check it carefully for holes and cut threads. Often these areas can be easily repaired. If it looks too damaged, or you aren't sure if you can darn or mend the damaged area, consider carefully whether it is worth purchasing or not.

Another idea is to buy used afghans that have been put together in sections or blocks, and carefully disman- tle the afghan. Keep the blocks or sections that you like or that are undamaged. It is very easy to sew the blocks or sections together again using yarn and a whip stitch to create a new afghan. Often you can find gently used afghans for less than the cost of new yarn, and if you are unable to knit or crochet your own, this is a simple way to provide one.

Bathroom Towel Set

A good quality set of bathroom towels that can be purchased on sale and have embellishments added to them, can also be a wonderful gift to set aside in the hope chest. White would be the practical color to get in these circumstances, since there is no way of knowing what color choice your daughter will make for her future bathroom. A beige or cream color could also be used as well. A future husband would probably not be happy with pink towels or bright yellow...so encourage your daughter to choose carefully.

For embellishments, the most common and beautiful ones are the hand crocheted or tatted lace sewn onto the towel. You can find a large assortment of beautiful pre-made lace in most fabric stores that would also work well. This lace has a similar look to the traditionally made heirloom ones but will save you a good deal of time and frustration if you are not proficient at crocheting or tatting. Ribbons are also a common embellishment and usually wash well. Adding a sprig of colored ribbon allows a plain white towel to be included in the color scheme of the bathroom. As was mentioned before, monogramming the towels, either yourself or having it done, offers simple elegance to the set. The rule for monogramming is the bride's initials are used for anything that is given to her prior to her marriage. Once she is married she takes on her husband's name, and then she receives monogramming initials using the letter of her new last name.

If ribbon or lace is too frilly for your daughter, plain monogrammed initials on the towel set is the best option. The thread color used for monogramming the initials usually matches the color of the towel, but you can use or request contrasting colors if you like. If you are not doing the monogramming yourself, most department stores will send the towels out to be monogrammed for you, but they will charge a per towel fee. You may also want to call sewing machine repair stores, tailor shops, bridal shops, and businesses that specialize in machine embroidery to find the best price.

When purchasing towels, the higher the thread count, the longer they wear. You can usually tell a good towel by the price, and by the feel, even before you find out the thread count. This is true for almost all linens. The looser weaves are more coarse to the touch with longer loops or fatter threads, and the price is much less. The tighter weaves are smoother, more uniform and have short even loops and a higher price tag. Loose weaves allow the fabric to be pulled and stretched easier during use and washing, and long loose loops will catch and pull out easily, creating a shortened life span for the towel or linen.

It is usually best to purchase the whole towel set at one time, in case the store stops offering that specific brand or color lot. It may be hard to match the set later, so think carefully before you purchase less than a full set. Long ago, the hope chest would not have been complete without "a dozen of everything" inside. Today, a minimum of four large bath towels, four hand towels, four washcloths and a bath mat are recommended. Shower curtains, accessories such as toilet seat covers, toilet tank covers, rugs to go beneath the sink and toilet, etc., can be purchased now or later. But the towel set, especially if it will be decorated, should be purchased first and in one complete set if at all possible.

A good quality set of towels can last your daughter for many, many years, and if time and care have added beautiful embellishments to them, they will be a special treat for her to use and display in her home.

Rugs

Braided or latch hook rugs can be made and placed inside your daughter's hope chest. There are kits or books with directions for making these, and there are many choices in colors and designs. A well-made braided throw rug can last through several decades of use if well cared for and it can be quickly repaired if it begins to unravel. These can be easy and inexpensive to make. If neutral colors are used, the rug can be used in almost any room of your daughter's future home.

Braided rugs can often be made with old, worn-out clothing or new calico fabrics, as well as plain or dyed muslin. 100% cotton is usually best; avoid any stretchy knitted fabrics as they will be hard to work with and will allow the rug to stretch and snag later.

Besides the designs and instructions for braided rugs, you may also be able to find booklet directions for making braided baskets and even braided bowls to match the braided rug. The baskets and bowls are not hard to make and will add a charm of their own to any room. These braided "rug, basket and bowl" sets can be made ahead for your daughter's bathroom, kitchen or nursery. If she already has colors in mind for what she would like her rooms to be, the braided items can be made with those color expectations in mind.

Multicolored fabrics used in these projects would allow a wider range of places for your daughter to use the items and would also allow her to change her color scheme when she needs or wants. If your daughter has not thought of colors yet, or wishes to wait until she is married to choose room colors, neutral colors can be used for the braided items, and they can be dyed later to match the color she finally chooses.

The rug sizes should be large enough to fit the area in which it will be used, but not overly large, which could cause a problem in a small apartment or home. A braided rug in the kitchen should be about the size you would find in a store-bought rug, one that would be placed in front of the sink or at the back door. The same would go for bathroom mats and rugs as well. Large oval or circular rugs that would be placed in the center of a room on linoleum or hardwood floors should be at least six feet in diameter. Anything smaller could give the rug a skimpy look.

Quilts

Quilts are an American heritage, and one that is always a welcome item in any home. There are thousands of quilt patterns and many ways make a quilt. Quilting has never lost its charm, and it is one needle-art that is, and always has been, very popular with young and old alike.

The bottom line for quilts is that they have the ability to change a house into a home. They soften the look of any room, making it a welcome haven for strangers, and they offer homey comfort for the family. They are an easy, functional and moveable decoration for any room.

The patterns and variations on quilts are endless, and they can be easily and inexpensively made with scraps of fabric or old clothing or from new fabrics. A quilt can be tailor-made to fit your daughter's preferences in color and design and enhance the other items she has made or set aside for the different rooms of her future home.

If creating a quilt for your daughter is not possible, there are beautiful quilts made here in the USA and also foreign imports that are quite affordable.

Quilts are one of the extra-special items that I will be giving to each of my children. I have friends and relatives who are unable to sew, either for physical reasons or because they have never learned. For mothers who are unable to sew, please don't be discouraged! I am including a section with options and ideas on how to provide a special quilt for your daughter without ever lifting a needle or plugging in the sewing machine!

What Belongs in a Hope Chest?

The Friendship Quilt

A Friendship Quilt or Album Quilt is very much like a Memory Quilt which I will discuss later, with a few exceptions. The blocks are usually all of the same size and often have the same pattern on each block if the block is pieced. Fabric can be used from the friend's own clothing to make it special, or from new fabric, but the same pattern design is usually followed throughout the entire quilt. In the middle of each block, the maker of the block either writes with a fabric pen or embroiders her name and the date onto the block. Some quilts even have favorite Bible verses, poems, sayings or heartfelt little notes written or embroidered on the block as well. The blocks are then sewn together, the quilt is quilted, and it is presented to the person for whom it was intended.

A friend of mine moved to the east coast in 1998. Before she moved, I asked her close friends to help me make a Friendship Quilt for her. We used 12-inch white muslin blocks for everyone to decorate in whatever way they wished. A few made their own block, making sure to fit the 12-inch size requirement. Each block was amazingly different and beautiful. One block had been decorated with apple stamps and fabric ink pads, and the names of each of the family members were written inside each apple. Another block had been decorated with embroidered flowers, while yet another had a large purple calico flower "glued" on with Tulip paints. Some blocks were pieced together or appliquéd by hand or machine. Each one was incredibly unique and special, as were the people who had made and signed them. When the blocks were all sewn together and the layers quilted together, the results were absolutely stunning!

On the back of the quilt, for each family that had made a block, we had each child in the family place a set of handprints on the white quilt back using either blue or pink fabric ink pads. For the infants and toddlers, we used their footprints instead of handprints. Each child's name and age went beneath his or her print. This was a wonderful addition to the quilt, and easily done.

This whole project was done in secret. My friend had no idea anyone was doing anything for her, so you can imagine the surprise and her tears as the curtains were drawn back from the window where the quilt had been hung, to show the full view for everyone. When she moved, the quilt and a little piece of each friend were taken with her. It now hangs from a wall in her home, and she remembers how blessed she was to have so many friends who loved her and created a lasting memory for her.

The Scrap Quilt

Scrap Quilts can be very colorful and a fun project

to make. There are hundreds of quilt patterns that can be used with scraps and dozens and dozens of books on the subject that are full of patterns. There is no lack of ideas in this area if you look for them. Most public libraries have large book sections on quilting because it is a very popular hobby for many women.

One interesting quilt that really doesn't need a pattern is the Crazy Quilt. Historians believe it came from the Victorian Era, though they have been around much longer than that I imagine. With these quilts, not only do you take the scraps and just "sew them together" whichever way you can make them fit, but the seams along the quilt top are covered with various embroidery stitches in all different colors which adds even more beauty and strength to the quilt.

The Crazy Quilt is usually a very colorful quilt and will not only perk up any room, but it is are relatively easy to make. Traditionally, deeper darker solid colors have been used, and velvet or corduroy was a favorite fabric to use. The embroidery flosses were lighter colors to contrast with the dark fabric, and no embroidery pattern was repeated on the quilt. With a hundred or more embroidery stitches over the entire top of the quilt, a Crazy Quilt is a wonderful way to learn and practice new embroidery stitches.

Of course you can make it any way you wish and with any kind of fabric, as well as using the same embroidery stitch for the entire top. It's all up to you.

The Hope Chest
The Theme Quilt

Theme Quilts can be any size and follow any theme or subject that you or your daughter enjoy. Are there favorite past-times or hobbies your family enjoys that would be fun to put onto a quilt? Gardening, favorite flowers, bird watching, bug collecting, horseback riding, sports, opera, music or instruments that are played at home, books, long car trips or vacations, church activities, special pets, daily walks, favorite Bible verses or hymns...there are so many different ideas and each one is thought up by you or your daughter, which makes this an absolutely unique "one-of-a-kind" quilt.

These are only examples to stimulate your thinking; the possibilities are limited only to your imagination. These quilts are usually small and fun to work on, and with today's wonderful selection of fabrics, anything is possible to make. Take a tour of your local fabric store if you have not been there lately. You will be amazed at what you see. Keepsake Quilting is a catalog company that offers a wide range of unusual and hard-to-find fabrics just for quilters and they are listed in the appendix. You can find fabrics with water or leaf designs, brick, stone, straw, grass, sky and stars, and fabric that dazzles the imagination.

Theme Quilts are something you can consider if you would like to send several different types of quilts with your daughter, or if you aren't sure what kind of quilt to make. Just look around your home for ideas and inspiration, and take a few days to notice what interests your daughter and can be used in a quilt.

There are also many kits that can be bought with the Theme Quilt in mind. Many have beautiful pictures to create and hang on the wall using a specific theme. Some fabric stores and quilt shops offer classes for those just starting. There are many options for you, just take a peek and see what appeals to you.

The Wedding Quilt

A Wedding Quilt has several aspects to it. It can be made by a mother for her daughter before her wedding, either in secret or with the daughter's knowledge and help in picking out the pattern and fabric. It can also be a quilt worked on by the mother and daughter together, as a final "blessing" or "good-bye" project. This can provide quiet times together, for both to reflect over the past years and say what is on their hearts.

A wedding quilt can also be made by several family members, either secretly or with the daughter's knowledge, but made specifically for her wedding. The Wedding Quilt will be the quilt that will grace the bridal bed in her new home and begin the start of her new life.

Whether made in secret or sewn with your daughter's help, this quilt will be special to your daughter on the day she is married, throughout many years of marriage and when she is a great-grandmother.

The Hope Chest

Baby Quilts

When I was growing up, some of the first quilts and afghans I made were baby-sized for my hope chest. This was good practice for me, and because they were smaller, I was able to finish them quickly and feel rewarded for the effort. This is an important aspect when a daughter is learning to sew. Start small and move on from there. It is very easy to become overwhelmed by large projects, especially when you are just learning. Small projects that are quickly and easily completed build confidence and give a sense of accomplishment and pride.

My daughters are learning embroidery by working on plain white fabric blocks. Pictures from coloring books have been traced onto them to use for the embroidery pattern. After the traced lines have been embroidered, the blocks are sewn together, with or without an intervening border between them. This makes a very cute baby quilt to place in the hope chest. I call these Colorbook Quilts. In this way children are starting small. They can learn how to trace designs onto fabric, embroider, sew, quilt and add binding all within a short period of time. Their hard effort is rewarded by a very sweet and beautiful quilt, and they are eager to start something else. One block at a time, one learning experience at a time, are the foundations that children can learn from, stand on and move forward with.

What Belongs in a Hope Chest?

During each of my pregnancies I have either made a Baby Quilt or crocheted a baby afghan especially for the newest blessing in our lives. As each child outgrew his or her quilt or afghan, I would place it inside my hope chest. One day, those afghans and quilts will be transferred to the child's own hope chest to be used for future grandchildren someday. Although still hard to fathom at this point in my life, I look forward to the day when my grandchildren are wrapped warm and snug in the same blanket their parents were wrapped in as infants and toddlers. And what a sweet sight to see grandbabies sleeping snugly cocooned in a quilt I have seen my daughter sew together piece by piece as a child. These will be special moments for any mother's heart!

Wall Hanging Quilts and Mini Quilts

Small Wall Hanging Quilts are a good way for daughters to learn and practice their sewing skills. These quilts are usually for the sole purpose of decoration. Consider using a favorite Bible verse and working around that to create a "picture" on the wall hanging. Or make a "Family Tree" by using appliqué to place a fabric tree onto the quilt top and then embroidering or using fabric ink pens to place all the names of ancestors on the limbs of the tree.

There are also many kits you can buy if you are worried about starting one of these quilts without a pattern or plan. And there are "Mini Quilts," often found in kits, or you can make one from a booklet. The Mini Quilt takes a common full-sized pattern and basically shrinks it. This allows you to make small, wall-sized quilts that are beautiful, and it gives you the opportunity to learn new quilting styles and techniques without the expense of making large, full-sized quilts.

Throw Quilt

These are more for practice and decorating purposes than actual use. As my daughters learn to sew on the sewing machine, a few of the smaller quilts that we make together will go into their hope chests. These little ones can be used to decorate their homes, to cover sleeping children on the sofa, or any number of other uses.

The Memory Quilt

A Memory Quilt, or Remembrance Quilt as it is called, is truly a unique and special gift. It is one of a kind and made with one specific person in mind. These quilts are not new; their roots go back hundreds of years and they are mentioned in the journals and diaries of women who had received them. The American version, the "Album Quilt," dates back to at least the 1840's.

Usually Memory Quilts were given to loved ones who were preparing to move away and most likely would never see their family and friends again. In the pioneer era, these quilts were sent with loved ones who made the long trek west by covered wagon. These quilts were often made from the clothing worn by those left behind. Using familiar clothing and fabrics helped the owner to "remember" their loved ones far away, which is where the quilt name came from. Aunt Abigail's purple velvet dress that she wore to church every Sunday would have part of the hem removed, and that piece of fabric would find its way into the Memory Quilt. Grandpa Henry's old red work shirt, that always had a button missing somewhere and had been mended countless times, would be cut up and included in the quilt. Perhaps his red shirt would be used as a work shirt on a man in the quilt or the center block in a log cabin square representing the "heart" or "hearth" of the home.

If there were no fabrics that could be used from family or friends' clothing, or if new fabric was used, the blocks themselves would be sewn in such a way as to remind the quilt owners of the people and places they had left behind. The log cabin design could represent the log home that the young lady had grown up in and left behind. The block could be complete with pine trees surrounding the home on the block, like the trees surrounding her childhood home. Appliquéd or embroidered crocus flowers could be sewn onto a block. This could help remind the young lady of the times she and her sisters had waited patiently through the long cold winter for those first brave little petals to be found growing out of clumps of snow.

Quilt blocks made from square pieces of different-colored fabrics might represent special Christmases, parties, church fellowships and favorite holidays. Each block of the quilt would be sewn with a specific idea or memory in mind, and each block had the maker's name embroidered on it somewhere. When all the blocks were complete, they would be sewn together to form the quilt top, and then it would be either quilted or tied down.

When the women would look at these quilts, far away in their new homes, the memories of their loved ones and all they left behind would come flooding back to them. This would be a bittersweet reminder of where they were, how far they had come and the loved ones who missed them. These quilts would be brought out and shown to children, with mother showing and re-minding the children from whom each scrap of fabric had come, what that person was like, any memories of the person and what each quilt block depicted or meant. In this way, mothers remembered and children learned their family heritage.

This is a lovely and endearing thought today, and with a little effort you can provide a link for your daughter that she can hold and show to her grandchil-dren. If you decide to make such a quilt, I would en-courage you to keep a notebook and fill it with informa-tion about the quilt. Even small samples of the fabrics used in the quilt could go into the notebook. On the first page, start with whom the quilt is for, who made the quilt, the date it was started and when it was finished. You can have one page or more dedicated for each block, and draw a picture of the block on the page. Then write down where the fabric for each block came from and any memories or history of that person or item. This will be an ongoing project that could cover many years. As each block is finished, simply add the information to the notebook.

The notebook can be as personalized as you would like. A few suggestions might be to have photos of your daughter at certain times throughout her life, while the blocks are being worked on and completed. A fun idea would be to include photos of the people wearing the clothing prior to its being cut and used for the quilt. Any photos you may have showing the blocks actually being created by you or family members would be a sweet addition to the notebook, too. The very final picture in the book might be of you, your daughter and the quilt. If there were several people involved in creating the quilt, a photo with everyone included would be a wonderful way to remember the time spent and the fun shared. It would be the perfect ending to a time-consuming project.

At the very beginning of my marriage, I began saving fabrics that were a part of our home. I put them aside, saving them for the specific purpose of making each child a Memory Quilt. Fabric from a shirt I made for their father has cows all over it, and the children learned to say "moooo" from it as babies. I have saved baby and toddler dresses that were worn to my father's funeral and to celebrate my younger brother's wedding. Scraps from baby and toddler clothes I made for each child have been saved. Even bits and pieces from my mother's scrap bag, leftovers from clothing she made for me as a child, have been set aside to be added to Memory Quilts.

Most books on quilting will tell you to use only 100% cotton, or fabrics that match in weight and thread counts. Memory Quilts are the one exception to the rule. ANYTHING goes with a Memory Quilt. It will not be for daily use but rather as something special that your daughter can pull out and look at or display in her home as a constant reminder of her youth and her dear family and friends.

When I have a few spare moments, I pull out the box that has these scraps of fabric hidden in them. I cut and sew and create the individual blocks for each child's quilt. I work on them either by hand or machine, and one day the blocks will all be sewn together for my children's Memory Quilt. There are still many more years ahead before my daughters are ready for marriage and still many more fabric memories to save. I will continue to make the blocks one by one and keep them safe. Sewing the blocks together and quilting the top of the quilt will be a joy, and a bittersweet time to remember the childhood left behind and the future ahead for each one.

What Belongs in a Hope Chest?

Memory Quilts are unique, inspired by the personality and memories of one specific person. A Memory Quilt made by a mother for her child can be created using a vast number of special memories or by starting at the beginning and moving forward in the child's life. The first block could represent the parents in some way, perhaps with a piece of the mother's wedding dress included in the block. Following could be a block representing the child's birth, homes the family lived in, the birth of siblings, family pets, vacations, new cars, special occasions, favorite childhood hobbies or toys, special Bible verses or sayings, favorite colors, or anything else that pertains to that particular child. The possibilities are endless and incredibly unique and personalized.

Here are a few ideas from my children's blocks. Using fabric inkpads and 8 inch blocks of white fabric, I have footprints or handprints from each of my children, with the child's name and the date under the print. These prints will be placed into each child's Memory Quilt. There are enough prints for each child to have their brothers' and sisters' prints also included in their quilt. One year we made paper snowflakes, cut out from small white with which paper that we decorated the windows of our home. Out of one hundred beautiful and unique snowflakes, I allowed each child to pick their very favorite, which I traced onto dark blue fabric using a chalk pencil. I embroidered the snowflake design with metallic silver thread for a very unique and stunning block. These blocks are very small, about

5 inches square.

Different-sized blocks brings up another point to these quilts. Each block can be the same size, or the blocks can be of varying sizes with borders of fabric added to the quilt block to eventually make them all the same size. These unique blocks can be sewn together to form the quilt top. The final size of my children's quilt blocks will be eight inches square. The fabric I use for the border on smaller blocks to reach the eight inch size will be from fabric that the child has worn or has memories of.

There is no limit to how large or how small to make the quilt. When I begin to sew all the blocks together, the number of blocks each child has will determine the size of the quilt.

For those who want to make a Memory Quilt for their daughter but have no scraps saved, it's never to late to start, so don't be discouraged! You can still make your daughter a beautiful Memory Quilt by using fabrics that your daughter has recently outgrown or that family, friends and relatives donate. If you have no clothing items to use following in the old tradition, the blocks can reflect different memories of family life using new fabrics. Just start and see where it leads you. You may find you only have enough fabric or time to make a small quilt, but a small quilt is better than no quilt and will still bring joy to your daughter. Use whatever is provided or you have on hand. Scrap lace and buttons can be used to enhance or make a design on a block, as well as any special emblem or iron-on transfer. If your daughter is on a ball team or other sports team, use one of her old jerseys with her name or number as the center for a block and add a border to it. Anything is possible.

Memory Quilts were also made from the clothing of a loved one who had died. With each piece of fabric lovingly cut and sewn together, it created a special way to remember that person.

When my husband's grandfather died in 1995, I requested whatever clothing the family did not want to give away to be sent to me. I ended up with several dress shirts, some T-shirts and dozens and dozens of ties. These were not the best fabric choices for making a quilt with as some were nylon and others 100% cotton. The fabrics were different thicknesses, and some were even stretchy knits as compared to woven fabric. But with this assorted fabric in hand, I was able to create a Memory Quilt for O'ma, his widow.

The dress shirt fabric was rather plain, dull and very thin. It was basic white and blue, but it made a good solid background for the ties which added a great deal of color. There were some T-shirts that had pictures or logos of the different clubs O'pa had been involved in, so I carefully cut those out and put a border of fabric around them to make a block. I was able to make several different blocks using the ties. One was a very large block that looked like a Dresden plate design, with the ties all laying next to each other and the slender ends leading towards the middle making a circle. On the middle block of the quilt, I embroidered the history behind the quilt, and why the quilt was made. Although the finished quilt was not large, only a lap sized quilt, my husband's grandmother was very happy to have something to snuggle with that had so many memories of her husband attached to it. When she needed to move several years later to live with her family, the quilt went with her.

There is a children's book called The Keeping Quilt by Patricia Polacco. It is the true story of a quilt that was handed down in her family. This is an endearing story about a family who leaves all they know and love behind in Russia to emigrate to America. This new country was very different from their homeland, and they missed their family back in Russia. When little Anna outgrows her dress and babushka, her mother says, "We will make a quilt to help us always remember home." So Anna's mother invited the neighborhood ladies to help cut the fabric and sew the quilt together. Uncle Vladimir's shirt, Aunt Havalah's nightdress and Aunt Natasha's apron all made their way into the quilt, and then Anna's brightly colored babushka was used for the border.

Through five generations this quilt was used to celebrate the family's life. Each wedding saw its use, for each birth it was used to wrap and welcome the new baby into the family, and when Anna died as a great-grandma it graced her bed. This same quilt welcomed the author, Patricia, into the family when she was born. The quilt is still being used by the author's family today.

She wrote "At night I would trace my fingers around the edges of each animal on the quilt before I went to sleep. I told mother stories about the animals on the quilt. She told me whose sleeve had made the horse, whose apron had made the chicken, whose dress had made the flowers, and whose babushka went around the quilt." I believe this story is one of the best examples of a Memory Quilt, and how much it can mean to those fortunate enough to use it.

This book would be a wonderful way to encourage you, your daughter, family members and friends to make a Memory Quilt. Throughout the book it shows how special the quilt is and how it is used and cherished. It is full of tradition, and each page is unique and beautiful in its own right. This book is still in print and can be found in nearly any library. If you need inspiration to get you going, read this book!

The thought of making a Memory Quilt may seem rather intimidating to some people, but it is actually a very easy thing to do. Even if you don't sew, there are many ways you can make blocks for one of these quilts and find someone who can sew it together for you. The effort you make now will one day be very appreciated by your daughter. Following are several suggestions for those of you who do not sew but feel led to make a Memory Quilt to bless your daughter.

The Hope Chest

The Last Word

Try to start some kind of quilt for your child, or at least put fabric aside for a quilt to be made in the future. Perhaps you will not be able to start the actual quilt making until she is betrothed, and the whole process can be a part of her wedding plans, or your gift to her. If you are not able to create a quilt either by yourself or with the help of others, then I am sure the Lord will lead you in other areas that your daughter will find joy and happiness in.

What Belongs in a Hope Chest?

Quilts for Non-Sewers

If you do not sew, or know anyone who can sew for you, there are still ways to provide a very special and personalized quilt for your daughter without ever lifting a needle. The following ideas are only suggestions to get you started, and you may find many different ways to make that special quilt on your own. Several of the ideas below can be used to make the quilt top, and once the top is done, you can contact a machine quilting business (look in your local phone book, in the back of quilting magazines, or ask at a fabric store for referrals). These companies are usually home based, or affiliated with fabric stores and will not only do the quilting for you, but add the binding to the edge of quilt as well. This will allow you to decorate the quilt top without ever having to use a needle or sewing machine.

The following are all simple examples and ideas for decorating a quilt top for your daughter. A few may require simple straight sewing on a machine. If you are unable to do this, someone from your church may be willing to do it for you, or you can hire someone to sew it within an hour or so. Take these ideas and make them fit your needs, and don't give up! Keep working and trying until you have found a way to provide a special quilt for your daughter, if that is what is on your heart.

There are now a large assortment of fabric markers

and ink pads that can be used on fabrics that are permanent and will not wash out. You can use these to decorate either plain or light colored fabrics. Some of these
can be washed out if you don't like the finished look,
and to make them permanent you simply iron the design on the block, which sets the ink onto the fabric
permanently. This gives you the option of how and
what to include on the fabric and to personalize them
in countless ways. If you make a mistake you can simply
wash it out and start over again.

There are tube paints that you can use to write,
draw or fill in large areas on fabric. These can usually be
found in craft or fabric stores in the embroidery section,
or through Herrschner's catalog which is listed in the
appendix. If you would like to use the tube paints or ink
pens, try using pictures or drawings from books as a pattern.

The easiest and cheapest way to copy a picture onto
fabric is to use the window method we have already
discussed. Simply tape a copy of the picture to a window. Then tape the fabric block on top of the picture
making sure to center it. With a pencil you can trace
the design onto the fabric in just a few minutes. Do this
during daylight hours as you need the light behind the
glass to be able to highlight the paper design for you.
This also works well if you need to put letters, names or
different writing fonts on the fabric.

To use different letters and fonts, use your computer
and find the font you like, type whatever wording you

need, and then print it and use this as the paper to hang in the window for tracing onto the fabric. This method works very well and is what I use exclusively instead of a light box. There are also numerous iron-on transfers that you can use as well, with tube paints or fabric pens.

Tulip paints are an easy way decorate a plain block or to glue layers of fabric together. Instead of using your sewing machine to appliqué a design onto a fabric block, you can apply a thick line of tulip paint along the seam of the appliquéd item and the block. This helps to form a glue-seal-seam of sorts when the paint dries.

Tulip paints come in a variety of colors in small bottles with tip ends and a cap. Some of these paints now have metallic glitter or are pearlized. By cutting patterns out from fabric, like a flower's petals, and placing the fabric onto the plain quilt block, you can then outline the edges of the fabric with the tulip paint and glue the layers together. Once the paint is dry, unless it is rubbed or pulled on a great deal, it will not peel off. If you choose this method, always hand wash the quilt in cool to warm water, and use caution that the quilt is not twisted or overly bent. Hang the quilt to dry, never use a clothes dryer. Try to find a place out of the sun to dry such as a porch area. The sun may heat the tulip paint enough to cause it to soften and bend away from the fabric, so a little care will prevent disaster. If at any point the paint begins to peel away from the fabric, simply apply a fabric glue to bind it once more to the fabric.

The Hope Chest

Picture transfer kits that can be bought at most craft and fabric stores will transfer a photo onto fabric. The process is somewhat messy, and you may want to practice with photos that are not important to you before you start to work on the irreplaceable ones. My sister-in-law, who is a non-sewer, has done this several times, and the results were wonderful. The process includes applying a gooey mixture over the photo, waiting a certain amount of time, and then placing the photo face down onto the fabric with a weight on top so the fabric can absorb the "goo" along with the picture. It is rather amazing to see the face of someone you know looking at you from a piece of fabric! My sister-in-law used this type of block to make a family history quilt and pillow shams to match. She found she could use a scanner and printer to copy the photos onto special photo paper, thus saving the original photo. What a wonderful idea! If you don't have a scanner or printer, you could take them to a photocopy store and ask to have them copied onto the special photo paper.

A quilting friend has also informed me that there are now computer programs that allow you to copy a picture directly onto fabric that is put through the printer like a piece of paper. This can provide incredibly personalized gifts for your daughter or anyone else in your family, and it is easily done. Just think of the possibilities

Another suggestion for non-sewers is to cut a large square, perhaps 10" x 10" or 12" x 12" blocks, from your daughter's outgrown skirts, dresses, the back of shirts or blouses, old sheets, curtains, clothing from brothers and sisters or mother and father, or other familiar fabrics. These large blocks can be easily sewn together to make one large quilt top. The blocks will also be colorful and bring back memories of the clothing your daughter wore growing up. This is very simple to make, and anyone with a basic idea of how to use a sewing machine can sew the top together in an hour or less. If you don't sew at all, a friend, neighbor or church member can easily sew the top together. Then you can send it off to be machine quilted, thereby creating a keepsake quilt for your daughter with very little effort.

Another twist on this idea is to use fabric from all the family members so that it will evoke a special memory for your daughter when she sees it and smoothes her hands over the fabric. Is there a fishing shirt that Dad always uses and she has fond memories of? A dress that you wore for a special occasion, her siblings' clothing or fabric used in your home for curtains or kitchen things? Any clothing from grandparents or other family members that can be used? Remember that just the fabric itself can bring back memories for your daughter even when she is a grandmother herself. Don't be so concerned about the size of this quilt; even a small-crib sized quilt is big enough for fond memories.

Before you cut up those out-grown children's clothing to make quilt blocks from, be sure you have a photo of that child wearing it, and if you missed the boat on that one, simply have the clothing "copied" onto acid-free paper at a scrapbook store. You'll have a photo of the "before" item to keep too...which can be shrunk to be smaller.

Renee Blokzyl

One more suggestion is to buy a large piece of white muslin, large enough to open and use for the ENTIRE quilt top. Muslin comes in several different widths, from 45 inches to 108 inches wide. You can also buy it in white, cream or its natural color. Wash, dry and iron your large piece of muslin, so it will be free from starches and dirt. Then you can decorate the entire top of the muslin any way you choose. If you do not pre-wash the fabric, be forewarned that you may have trouble from the starch applied at the fabric mill. It will prevent any ink, paint, glue or other embellishment from adhering to the fabric, and with the first washing you will lose most of your hard work in the wash water.

One-piece quilt tops were very popular in the 1500 - 1700's. They were heavily quilted in spectacular designs, for the decoration, and the stitching was often so close together that the quilt had very little wear to it. Several of these quilts can be found in museums, and they are in wonderful condition for their age.

A suggestion for the one-piece quilt would be to have a family history drawn or colored onto the fabric. A huge tree with off-shooting branches in the middle of the quilt top would make a wonderful place to list the lineage on. By using fabric paints or markers, you can color pictures, add names, dates or other information and make it a very beautiful quilt top.

Another idea would be to allow each family member or friend to decorate a designated area of the muslin top any way they wish and to sign that area and date it.

Purchasing the muslin while your daughter is still quite young would allow you to bring it out for each birthday. Your daughter could draw or decorate one small area each year until the muslin is full. Siblings, family and friends could also help decorate the quilt top as well. This is a sweet quilt that she will cherish, and have many happy memories associated with. When the quilt top is filled, simply send it off to be machine quilted and the binding placed on the edges, and you have a very special and unique quilt for your daughter. Whether the mother, father, grandparents or the daughter herself decide to do this type of quilt, it is easily done and makes a wonderful treasure to add to the hope chest.

The one-piece quilt is also a very special gift to keep in mind for friends, family or other special people. Very simple, easily done, but it has a very lasting and endearing quality...and NO sewing!

If you would like to include a quilt, but simply can't make one yourself or find someone to make one for you, there is one more alternative. Buy a pre-made quilt from a department store, one that has a white or light

The Hope Chest

colored background. On the back of the quilt, using fabric paints, fabric markers or fabric ink pads, allow those who are close to your daughter's heart to make their handprints. Beneath their handprint, they should sign their name and add the date with a fabric marker. Remember to iron the ink if it needs heat to set it permanently. This will still be a sweet gift and one that is personalized. These also make wonderful gifts for friends or family members who are moving if you can't sew a quilt yourself, or don't have the time. A quilt made this way makes a nice gift for baby showers, bridal showers and school teachers. These are quick and can be done in one afternoon if everyone is able to decorate their allotted area in a timely manner.

Cradles

Cradles are an intricate part of history, and they can be found throughout the ages in reference to the blessing of children in a marriage and the continuance of a country's future. Just the sight of a cradle will bring many women fond memories of their own babies, who are now grown. Cradles are the age-old symbol of innocent infancy, and that hold the future within their rocking arms.

When I became engaged to my husband, my father wanted to make something special for me as a wedding gift. He had already supplied me with a wonderful hope chest, so he began trying to think of something he could make that would be extra special. He remembered how I had always wanted a wooden cradle for my dolls as a child, and so he quietly and carefully began to build a solid maple cradle, in the style of the pilgrim cradles, in his workshop. At my wedding he presented me with this very special gift, and it was truly the best wedding present that had been given to us, because it was a promise of future blessings to come.

He lived long enough to see two of my seven children sleep inside the cradle he had so lovingly created. And as a legacy to him, I have placed a small brass plaque on the bottom of the cradle with the history behind its existence. This includes his name, the date of our wedding with both my name and my husband's name. Successive small plaques for each child who has slept inside are also placed beneath the cradle. In the future, as each grandchild is born and takes his or her turn sleeping inside, another plaque will be added to the bottom as an on-going family tree is created beneath the cradle.

Since I have seven children, there is no practical way for this one cradle to be passed down to each child. My husband will build a cradle for each daughter or daughter-in-law as a wedding gift, and I hope to be able to carry on the tradition my father started. This original cradle will go to one of my children, just as my mother's sewing machine and my own hope chest will go to my other children.

The Hope Chest

The hope chest, like the cradle, will have a small plaque attached inside with its history and all the successive owners names engraved within.

What Belongs in a Hope Chest?

Baby Items

A hope chest may or may not include baby items. This is up to the parents' discretion and judgment and the daughter's wishes. For those who wish to include baby items in the hope chest, there are many items to choose from and many ways of decorating the individual pieces. If you and your daughter feel led to prepare baby items to place in her hope chest for future use, start by making a list of the items and the sizes you will make. This will be an important help to you.

Ask yourself whether you will simply make a few baby blankets or a whole layette set. Will you use white, green, yellow or cream colors for future blessings, or will you use blue, pink or both together? Will they be simple practical items or will they be heirloom quality that can be handed down for your great-grandchildren to use? What types of fabric will you use: printed calico or flannel, plain muslin or dotted Swiss, Irish linen or batiste? Will you use smocking, hardanger, embroidery, crochet, cross stitch, ribbon embroidery or something else for embellishment, or will the items be very plain? What sizes will you make: newborn, 3-6 months, 6-9 months, 9-12 months...will anything be made for toddlers?

Baby blankets, quilts and afghans are easy to make and are usually a standard size. A generous size for baby blankets would be 45 inches by 45 inches. This may seem large for a newborn, but he or she will quickly outgrow the small blankets within a few weeks or months, and the larger ones will still be in use when the baby is a toddler. A minimum of 6 skeins of 4-ply yarn will give a good-sized afghan depending on the size of your stitching and the pattern you choose. If afghans are made of white yarn, colored ribbons can be woven through the afghan. The ribbon can be changed for either boys or girls in the future.

If you are planning on making baby items, white is the best choice since there is no way of knowing whether future babies will be boys or girls. Also, if possible, try to match all the items together by using the same fabric, lace or buttons for the baby clothes. If a printed fabric is used, buy extra fabric and place any leftovers in the hope chest. The extra fabric can be used later to add decorative touches to the nursery. Ties for the curtains, cushions for the rocking chair, or a lampshade covering can be created from the matching fabric. Extra fabric can also be used on or with store-bought items, which will allow the whole room to blend together. And don't forget to keep a little swatch of fabric to add to the baby book.

It is usually recommended that baby booties, hats and sweaters should be sized for either newborn or 6-9-month-old babies. Bibs can be made for drooling babies (3-9 months) or for babies who are eating solid foods

What Belongs in a Hope Chest?

(6+ months). Bibs can be made in a wide variety of ways and with several kinds of fabric choices. The most commonly seen are the ones made from terry-cloth fabric with either a binding or satin stitching around the entire edge of the bib. 100% cotton in white, or a solid pastel color is a popular choice. Pre-quilted fabrics with cloth on one side and batting on the other, are very easy to use, and they make absorbent bibs.

For food bibs, darker colors hide stains better, so an assortment of dark bibs would hold up through multiple children, and the new mother will not have to worry about laundering them and preventing stains.

If you are making your own bibs, especially drool bibs, take the time to double the fabric for extra absorbency. Cross stitch, embroidery, crocheting, hardanger, quilting, ribbon embroidery and tube paints are the more common ways of embellishing bibs. Drool bibs for the most part do not get stained or worn out easily and can be passed down through generations. Making several special bibs using heirloom sewing techniques and fine linen and fabric is a wonderful way to start a new tradition, though it may be years before you see them used.

These are just a few basic ideas. If you and your daughter would like to prepare in this area, there are many beautiful items that can be created and almost too many patterns and designs to choose from! For those who wish to wait until your daughter is married and expecting ,there will be joy in planning for the new baby's arrival at a future date. This area depends on your heart and your own judgment.

It would also be a blessing to include your daughter's grandmother in these projects if she has an interest. Most grandmothers have made baby items through the years for their own children, and then for their grandchildren. Grandmothers may enjoy helping with an item or two, or with the whole set.

> I've asked my mother-in-law to knit special baby blankets for future generations NOW. This may sound silly, but she complains that she hasn't anything to knit at times and I thought that maybe, just maybe my children could have one specially made for them to put away, from Grandma, to use someday. As she is getting older and anything is possible, I want them to have her in their lives whether she is here or not. And she will be kept busy working with loving hands preparing for her future great-grandchildren. She might go further yet, imagine my girls having a baby outfit with booties to match waiting in their hope chests for their future children if God wills it for them…
>
> Renee Blokzyl

Using an item that was made by a grandmother or aunt is a lovely way for your daughter to treasure her past while using it in the present. It also allows your daughter's children a link to their past, as often the great-grandparents are gone before the child is old enough to remember them.

What Belongs in a Hope Chest?

Each child has something handmade by Nannie, even our youngest who will be six years old in two weeks. When Faith was born, Nannie was almost 96, struggling to see clearly, and yet wanted to make something for her, to impart a piece of herself. Faith still wears a nightgown Nannie made for her, which was made in a size 6 while Faith was still a baby. It was, I think, her way of sending a part of herself into the future, for us to remember her by. And I must also tell you that all her sewing was done on a treadle sewing machine. She said that electric machines always got away from her.

Merri Williams

If your daughter is already engaged or betrothed, and time is short, grandmothers or older aunts can help prepare items for the hope chest, working alongside your daughter. "Many hands make light work" is a wonderful saying, especially when time is closing in and there is still much to do.

The Hope Chest

Practical Items

Here we find items that your daughter will need and may use almost daily in her future life. These can be accumulated over time and set aside for her. Some items your daughter may actually be using prior to her marriage. The following items are only a few examples. Your heart will be your true guide in this area, and remember that the best hope chest you can give your child is the knowledge she takes with her. If you set aside an item for her, make sure she knows how to use it to full advantage.

Sewing Machine and Accessories

A basic sewing machine that can sew a straight running stitch, zigzag stitch, hem stitch, buttonhole stitch and blind stitch is a good start for any young lady learning to sew. With this basic machine, she can learn to do almost anything. Any other machine you may have or she may acquire, such as a serger or embroidery machine, will enhance the skills she learned using the basic sewing machine.

Accessories could include a sewing machine table with drawers to store her machine and all the parts and accessories. Any special equipment or attachments for the basic sewing machine should be considered; a ruffler-gatherer or a quilting foot are two common attachments that she might find useful. Other useful items are cutting board to go on top of a table to help prevent damage to the table; an ironing board, either a full-sized one or a shorter tabletop board and a good pair of sturdy stainless steel scissors are almost critical if your daughter plans on any sewing in the future. These will be high priced, but the hard steel will hold up for decades and can be re-targeted as needed. Cheaper scissors are usually only good for one to two projects and can not be re-sharpened. The metal used in the cheaper scissors is a soft metal which bends and dents easily.

Pinking shears are also a useful item if your daughter will be doing a lot of sewing. Pinking shears are used to help keep seam edges from unraveling, and they have been used long before sergers appeared to do a similar job. A set of pinking shears would be a wise investment unless there are plans to secure a serger for your daughter in the future. Many other accessories can be included if they are desired.

If you make a large investment in a sewing machine, it would be wise to make sure your daughter wants one and to have your daughter learn to use it. I attended a wedding where the bride and groom opened their wedding gifts in front of their guests. The bride could barely contain her disappointment when she opened a large beautifully wrapped gift from her grandmother. When she lifted the gift up for all the guests to see, those of us who were sewers nearly gasped at the highly priced, top-of-the-line sewing machine that she held. Over the next two years, that young lady never once opened the box to even take a peek, and she finally sold it at a garage sale still unopened. The moral of the story is, choose carefully what your daughter will want, need and use!

Sewing Basket and Accessories

Whether your daughter is blessed with a sewing machine or not, a sturdy well-stocked sewing basket is a must. Even if she does not sew, she may still have a need for thread, needles, patches and other common items. It's much easier to repair something as soon as you notice it needs attention, than to try to mend a big pile that has stacked up over time.

There are so many beautiful sewing baskets today, available in all price ranges, that it may be hard to choose just one! There is also a wide variety of sizes to choose from, and your daughter may end up with more than one basket.

I have one basket that my mother gave me when I was five years old. It's a large, rectangular, old wicker picnic basket. She spray painted the basket with gold paint inside and out. It has little wicker latches on the front and two handles as well. I learned to hand sew using this basket, and it now holds all my laces, ribbons, zippers and buttons. This basket is nothing special, and probably wouldn't even sell at a garage sale, but it has lasted through over 30 years of use and is still strong and able to hold a great deal of items.

I also have a sewing basket that holds all my embroidery floss, hoops and needles. This was a gift from my mother for my thirteenth birthday. My mother had stocked it well with supplies and had several re-shaped pillowcases inside for me to work on. This one is still used for my embroidery, and has many memories attached to it.

The third sewing basket I have is made of solid wood. This is the sturdiest sewing basket I own and bought on sale for half price. When one of the little hinges broke, it was fairly easy to replace it. Because there is one large middle section and six smaller side trays that pull out in tiers, I can keep all my regular sewing supplies in this one basket. All the items I would need to repair a missing button or to mend a tear are kept in this basket. It has a pleasing look as well, so I keep it out for quick use and also to add a homey look to our front room.

Yet another basket I have is for yarn and crochet hooks. This one has two wood handles and the rest is made from tapestry fabric. There is a large over-sized pocket on the outside, and another on the inside to store my needles and patterns. This would be excellent for either crocheting or knitting, and holds enough yarn for even large projects.

The most common basket used is the one for regular sewing. It will be used far more often than the others. If you are limited in funds, keep your eyes open at thrift stores and garage sales for a simple basket that has a lid. You can either add a lining to it or leave it as-is. Even a simple basket can bless your daughter, and it's what's inside the basket and your daughter's heart that is important, not how much was spent on a beautiful new, showy one. She can always have her sewing basket upgraded to a nicer one at some future point, but in the meantime she will be able to use and care for the simple one she started with.

If you are unable to find an appropriate basket to use, or would like something really sturdy for a younger child, consider decorative tins. Cookie and candy tins left over from Christmas make wonderful sewing containers and can be decoupage if the outside is not pleasing. The inside can be worked in such a way that flannel or corduroy fabric can be glued in place, and there are stuffed pillowed areas for securing needles and pins.

What is to be put inside the sewing basket? Here is a list of items that would be included in a well-stocked sewing basket:

Spools of thread - in the more common colors,
    at least a dozen minimum
Scissors - good quality pair of hard steel
Trimming Scissors - smaller pointed tip scissors
Seam ripper
Sewing gauge
Tape measure
Tracing paper & wheel

What Belongs in a Hope Chest?

Wide assortment of needles - a needle case would be
    a nice addition
Glass headed silk pins - will NOT cause runs in fabric,
    excellent choice!
Pincushion with needle sharpener
Iron on patches and mending tape
Stitch Witchery
Assorted snaps
Hook & eyes
Metal tin box or glass jar - for assorted buttons
Needle threader
Chalk pencil - for marking
Skeins of embroidery thread - multiple colors
Embroidery hoop
Sweater repair hook - to repair snagged knitted items
Assorted sizes of safety pins

Crochet and Knitting Items

Rosewood, walnut or beech wood crochet hooks
and knitting needles have a wonderful feel to them as
they slide through your fingers creating many wonder-

wonderful articles for a family's use. These are heirloom quality and will outlast your daughter to be passed on to her grandchildren some day. They are usually very high-priced, unless you happen to find them on sale or rescue them from an antique or thrift store. You may also come across ivory or bone hooks and knitting needles as well. These too make wonderful heirloom treasures that bring joy and contentment when used.

My daughters have each received a complete set of steel crochet hooks and a zippered case to keep them in. As they grow older, they will receive a few of the hardwood hooks and needles to add to their collection of steel ones.

If your daughter enjoys knitting or crocheting, you might want to provide a knitting basket or crochet basket for her that includes items she would need. These might include knitting needles, crochet hooks, a stitch gauge, a small pair of good quality scissors, books or booklets with the basic stitches and instructions for articles to make and of course, yarn!

What Belongs in a Hope Chest?

Kitchen and Cooking Items

We use cast iron for our cooking, and it seems as if nothing cooks better meals than our huge cast iron Dutch oven simmering away on the stovetop. If cared for properly, they can last for decades. I learned to cook using cast iron frying pans and griddles, and my daughters have learned to cook the same way. Included in my daughters' hope chests will be a set of cast iron frying pans in three sizes, a large cast iron griddle and a smaller Dutch oven.

You and your daughter may want to include a set of cookware in her hope chest. Or you may want to include even more, like a set of stock pots, baking dishes, muffin pans, bread pans, cake and pie pans, cookie sheets, casserole dishes, Pyrex mixing bowls, mixing cups and measuring spoons as well as other kitchenware.

If possible, depending on finances, I would like to bless each of my children with a large heavy-duty mixer like a Bosch or Kitchen Aid and many of the attachments that would go with them. I am looking at garage sales, thrift stores and in the local newspapers for these items. Just like the sewing machine mentioned previously, some brides receive items like a Bosch mixer that they have no idea how to use, and they sell it cheaply or give it away to charity. You would be surprised what you can find by watching and waiting.

The Hope Chest

Our family usually cans food during the summer and fall months, putting jars and jars of vegetables, fruits and jams on the shelf for winter and spring. One more item that I will include in my daughters hope chests will be a pressure canner that holds seven quart jars at once. Not only will they be able to can vegetables with the canner, but they can use it as a pressure cooker as well.

Several boxes of canning jars will also be set aside for my daughters. I purchase these at the end of the summer when they go on sale. Buy quarts, pints and half-pints, a dozen jars per box, and they will have a good start on putting food on their shelves and saving money in the process. Canning accessories can also be bought at the end of summer on clearance.

Are there any kitchen items that you would like to send with your daughter? Anything that your family specializes in and she could start using in her new home to keep the tradition going? One family I know makes homemade noodles and has a wonderful pasta machine. They have become experts in noodle making, and they make all types and styles of noodles. Not only does their machine shoot out the noodles sliced and ready to hang up to dry, but they have a very old hardwood noodle cutter that is the funniest thing you could see. It's round like a long thin spindle and has raised cutting ridges carved out with a lathe around the spindle. Although they don't use this for their noodle making, each of their children has played with it to "practice" making noodles, keeping themselves busy while the parents used the machine to finish the edible noodles. This little noodle maker hangs on a peg in the kitchen, and it holds many fond memories for the children. Their daughter is looking forward to a pasta maker for her hope chest so she can prepare the same delicious meals for her new husband as she has eaten at home with her family. She has made her mother promise to give her the hardwood noodle maker as a baby gift for the first grandchild!

There are so many kitchen accessories that a young lady needs when she is newly married. Some of those items are often given as wedding presents, but many of the unusual or family favorites may not be given to her. Think about this aspect of the hope chest for awhile, and write down any ideas that come to you. Ask your daughter what her thoughts are on this; my own daughters often come up with suggestions that I had never considered before. As we peruse garage sales, thrift stores and antique shops together, they are always on the lookout for items to put into their hope chests.

Medical and Herbal Supplies

Every home should have a complete first aid kit, but even more important is knowing how to give first aid. While your daughter is in her teen years, attend a first aid and CPR class with her at your local Red Cross. This takes only a few hours, but the knowledge will last a lifetime. As a former Emergency Room nurse, I know that a basic knowledge of first aid and CPR can provide those precious moments needed to get professional help to someone...and that life may be someone you love. Make the time, and do it together.

There are many first aid kits available to purchase, or you can create your own kit, which is more cost-effective and better-equipped. A good first aid book will list what you would want to have on hand, but think further ahead than that. What about over-the-counter medications that you could add, thereby reducing the cost of what your daughter will need to invest in when she starts her new home? Consider including regular medications like Tylenol, Advil, cold and cough remedies, laxatives, anti-diarrhea medication, Visine or other eye drops, antacid medications, allergy medications and any others you think could be needed or used. If you decide to include anything that has an expiration date, make a list of the items you would like to include, then wait until your daughter has a wedding date planned before purchasing anything. This way nothing will expire before your daughter has a chance to use it.

If you plan on creating your own first aid kit, the best container to use is a larger fishing tackle box. These types of containers are what most paramedic and ambulance units use. They are strong, tough, portable, hold a large number of items and have a long life expectancy. We have one that has a top and bottom half. . The top half pulls up and out on each side, exposing three tiered trays with compartments. In the bottom half you can place anything large that won't fit on the trays. It is easily portable and fits into most closets or cabinets for easy accessibility. These are inexpensive at most department or discount stores.

Today herbal remedies are gaining in popularity as a natural treatment for assorted illnesses and conditions. Some families rely solely on diet and herbal treatments. Whether you use only a few select natural products or rely on them completely, consider starting a small journal, recipe card file or a small notebook about what has worked for your family and what advice you would like to pass along to your daughter. You never know when your daughter may need the information, or whether you will be available to call in an emergency for her to ask questions. If it's written out, she will have the information handy whenever it's needed. What are some of those wonderful homemade cures that your mother learned from her mother who learned from her mother? This was once knowledge that every bride took with her to her new home.

Many old cures can bring instant comfort and help avoid trips to the doctor. But if you don't write them down they can be forgotten or confused and will be of no use when they are needed. On a simple index card list the ailment and the cure, and place these in your daughter's recipe box for easy access under the heading "Home Cures."

An herbal "first aid kit" for your daughter's new

home may be something you would want to think about putting together when a wedding date has been chosen so the items would not sit for a long period of time or expire before her wedding. This can be an expensive hope chest item to include, but if you feel she should have it, then plan ahead and make your list of the items you would like to include. Remember to write down the information to go along with the kit, or purchase a book that you rely on yourself.

Home Repair Equipment

This would be a good area for your husband or a grandfather to get involved, although you should keep an ongoing list of items that you find handy to have within reach, too. Small screwdrivers, hammers and pliers would be nice to have nearby in a small toolbox. Other useful items would be assorted sizes of nails, screws, picture hanging attachments, duct tape, a toilet plunger, measuring tape, small level, stud-finder to find the 2x4's in walls, electrical tape, fire extinguisher, battery operated smoke alarms, a flashlight, a book on simple home repairs, assorted batteries in different sizes and anything else you think might be handy.

A small toolbox and fire extinguisher could easily find a place beneath the kitchen sink in your daughter's future home, and they will be within quick reach for any repair that might be needed. Even if your future son-in-law is handy with tools and has a large assort-

What Belongs in a Hope Chest?

ment himself, it is far easier for a wife to have a small stash of tools nearby so she does not have to sort through her husband's tools to find what she needs.

Furniture and Home Accessories

Furniture may be an odd item to include in a hope chest, as most pieces of furniture are too large to actually put inside the chest, but don't overlook this item as one that your daughter will enjoy having ready for her new home.

The furniture items don't need to be large, elaborate or expensive. A small bookshelf for her books, a small shelf to place her tea cups and saucers, the dresser she grew up with and that has always held her clothes, a framed mirror or table lamp will be appreciated. Large items such as a bed frame, or even her piano if she plays, could be considered. A sturdy rocking chair is nearly a necessity in any comfortable home. How nice it would be to have a small side table next to the rocker to place a drink or lamp on while she rocks her future babies to sleep.

A smart bride and groom will realize it is far better to start off their married lives without the added debt burden of new furniture and will be gracious and happy to receive gently used items from family and friends. Over the years, the thrill of saving and purchasing furniture items that they have chosen, will mean far more to them than if they bought a whole houseful of new items and worked for years to pay off the debt. Consider this as your daughter is in her teen years - you may find it a good way to rid yourself of unwanted furniture items. If those items were stored for several years until she is ready for them, this would be a wonderful addition for her new home, with happy links to her childhood as well. If she and her new husband decide they can't take your stored items, it's simple enough to donate them to a needy cause. Either way, they will be put to good use.

Grandparents often downsize their homes as they get older. If your daughter's grandparents decide to move from a larger home to a smaller one, ask if you can have some of the items they won't be able to take with them. Older generations tend to purchase good-quality, long-lasting items that your daughter will be able to use for years. Old sofas have sturdy wood construction and with new upholstery will last for decades, unlike the modern foam-cushioned sofas that wear out after a year or two. Old solid wood furniture is a better choice than the newer veneered version, and if your daughter is not fond of the color of the items, she can paint them or strip off the old varnish and re-stain them.

Keep these ideas fresh in your mind when you hear of friends and family who are moving, or if you see an estate sale or moving sale nearby. As your daughter goes through her teen years, a few items here and there may

What Belongs in a Hope Chest?

end up furnishing her entire home when she is married, saving her thousands of dollars.

If you have no storage available, or very little storage space, look into the space rentals at storage lots. There are several different space sizes you can rent, and you may find that it will be handy not only to put aside your daughter's larger items but the overflow from your own home as well.

Favorite Childhood Toys, Clothes and Personal Articles

Do you have any special baby clothes or baby toys that you have saved, simply because the sight of them brings back fond memories? That little baby rattle that your daughter cut her first teeth on so long ago. The hand-crocheted baby sweater that your great aunt made for your daughter that was so soft it felt like it was spun of misty clouds. Or the baby blankie that she wore out and you thought she would never outgrow. Memories are in everything that touches our lives. Some items are nothing special, but some are nearly irreplaceable. Do you have these memories tucked away in a special place? I do!

In my daughter's hope chests there will be a few special baby clothes that were given to them when they were born. These are from their grandparents or other close family or friends, and they can be handed down to their children. I have a soft, fluffy yellow baby sweater that was a gift from my uncle when I was born. Each of my daughters has worn this when they were tiny, and one day I hope their children will wear it. Another gift that will be handed down is a beautiful hand-crocheted infant bib that was made for one of my children by a dear lady who used her own mother's antique infant bib as a pattern. She copied the stitches and created a new heirloom for my family. I plan on making my grand-children a bib using that same pattern.

The same thought applies to baby toys and toys from their childhood. Each child has those "special" toys that they slept with each night, or played with until all the fuzz came off the teddy bear or the doll's hair was a mass of tangled knots. A mother knows which toys were special to her children, which ones they asked for when sick or hurt, which books were asked to be read over and over and over again. These are the special ones that should be set aside and kept for your daughter. Once she has outgrown them, hide them away so they will not be lost or damaged. They can be presented to her when she is given her hope chest, or later when she is married and expecting your first grandchild.

Mama finished a needlepoint picture of a girl praying, with the prayer "Now I Lay Me Down To Sleep," when my daughter was born. She had started that picture 30 years earlier when I was born and never finished it until her grand-daughter was born. That was a gift for our daugh-ter and me at the same time, and I delight in it every time I walk down the hall. When our son was born, Mama embroidered a beautiful little baby's pillow for him, which he nearly wore out before he agreed to let me put it away when he was about 3 years old. I carefully washed it the last time and packed it in its own little box. He will remember it clearly when he sees it again a few years from now, and it will bring him delight once more."

Joan Taylor

My daughters get a chuckle out of the only toy I have left from my childhood, an old worn frazzled teddy bear I was given by my older brother when I was brought home from the hospital. This little bear sports the very first stitching I ever attempted beneath its chin, and which I was extremely proud of as a seven-year-old. It has also been permanently stained on the white area inside its ears, by blue chalk that I rubbed on when I tried to match it to the blue dress I had dressed it in as a child. I must have been seven or eight at the time, but after all these years, the blue chalk is still imbedded in those old ears and the story delights my children every time they ask me to tell it. "Mommy" was actually a little child once too, and that teddy bear proves it! It is a link to my past that my children cherish.

The Hope Chest

My Mom surprised me at my wedding shower by giving me a beautiful chest. It wasn't very large as it wasn't filled with items for my home but it held childhood treasures. My first pair of ice skates, school papers and report cards, notes and various other things...

Cindy McCarthy

What are some childhood treasures your daughter holds close to her heart? Would she enjoy showing them to her own children and watching them play with them? Think before you throw away her childhood treasures; once they are gone there is no way to get them back, and one day they may mean a great deal to her. Even now, I often wonder just what happened to certain childhood toys that I have fond memories of. I know "I" didn't throw them away, so who did?

A Child's Scrapbook

Baby books are such a wonderful way to keep all those memories ready to be brought to the forefront of our minds with the flip of a page. Yet once children are past the baby and toddler stages, how many mothers bother to continue on with those wonderful insights and collections of youth? We get SO busy, have too many things to keep up with, that those little milestones in a child's life are thrown by the wayside after our children can walk and talk.

A scrapbook for your daughter, including pictures she has drawn, music she has played, awards she has won, experiments she has worked on in school, book reports, report cards, locks of hair, pictures of her throughout her growing up years, pictures of her first bicycle and her first car...there are too many things that can be collected not to make an attempt at scrapbooking them together. If all you do is to toss these things into a small shoebox, with a name and date on the back, then years later when you DO have the time, it will be much easier to unravel all the details and present your daughter with a wonderful childhood memory scrapbook! And the secret is, it only takes a few seconds to put these things aside for her. You will be thankful you did years from now.

There are so many priceless treasures that our children hand to us each day that we ought to make the effort of collecting them, along with any little explanations like "this is a cat" under the little blob of crayon marks. Or place each person's name under their picture when your children start drawing their family portraits at about age three or four. I have several renditions of my children's family portraits framed and on the wall, with each person's name written under their drawn picture and one even has "Mommy holding the new baby" in it. These were just too precious for me to simply toss away.

A child's heart comes through in her drawing, even

if it is only simple stick figures or elaborate and colorful full-sized pictures!

> ...my five-year old loves everything he draws (even the multitudinous pages with one line down the middle!), he always "shares" flamboyant explanations and expressions of absolute rapture over his pictures. My little three-year-old enjoys filling his paintings to the brim with color, and letting that say almost all.....except for heart-catching little things, like his explanation of a painting with black at one end, covered with a rich moss green, except for a red patch in the middle...quite well balanced...and he just quietly said, "It's Jesus' Love," and kept on painting.

> Lorraine Nessman

How many of these treasures have we already thrown away, sometimes on a daily basis because we don't want to clutter our homes? Yet what a simple and sweet explanation from a child's heart about one of the most complex aspects of Christianity...to explain "Jesus's Love." This mother will never be able to look at this picture without remembering her child's sweet face and that simple explanation of Love. This is precious! This is a keeper! Do you have any keepers at home?

Take the time to tuck these little things away in a file folder or shoebox with a note on the back and the date, and which child created it. As you or your child go through pages of these little treasures in the future, it can bring back many wonderful memories. Older children find joy in their simple earlier drawings. Often they will remember when they drew them and may even be able to verbally expand on the picture they had drawn long ago, when they were too young to have a big enough vocabulary to explain it.

Besides a general scrapbook, you can also make special scrapbooks for one specific area. Paintings, drawings, music, awards, memorized Bible verses, stories they have written, book reports they have written, Sunday School projects...whatever you are motivated to keep for each child

My youngest daughter has artistic talent, and I have several books filled with her work. I have pictures she began to draw at age two progressing to her current age, all with her name and the approximate date they were made. Even now she and I both enjoy going through them and remembering all her little pictures, and I marvel at how she has progressed through the years.

My middle daughter is very talented on the piano and violin, and I have made copies of the favorite songs she has played through the years, her piano recital sheet music and even her piano teacher's notes in a special book for her.

My oldest enjoys writing, and has begun to write short stories. These stories, along with anything else she writes, will be placed inside her special scrapbook for her to have when she is grown.

If you create a scrapbook for your children, mark

the dates on the items that go inside as well as your child's name if you have more than one child. It's very easy years later to wonder which child made what picture, what piece of music was played for which recital, and so forth. Also, if you desire a copy of the items that go into your daughter's scrapbook, copy them and create a scrapbook for yourself. I have been doing this, as well as taking items that don't fit or that they have an excess of in their own books and placing them in my "Mommy Scrapbook." One day, when my children are grown and gone, I will still be able to sit down and flip through several thick "Mommy" scrapbooks. What a wonderful way to remember their sweet childhood days and the special little lives that God had placed into my life.

If you don't have the time to place everything into a scrapbook now, at least set aside items so they are available when you are ready to start on this project. If you put them in a cardboard box, make sure it is kept in a safe place away from water, is easily accessible so you can continually add items and is plainly marked NOT to throw away!

One dear mother I know uses every Thursday night to sit at her kitchen table and work on some kind of scrapbook or photo album. In this way she is able to take her stacks of papers and photos and place them safely between pages. This allows her to keep her home free from stacks of papers and boxes of photos that are so easy to lose track of.

What Belongs in a Hope Chest?

With Creative Memories and the generic brands found in most department and craft stores, the acid-free paper, stickers, albums and the equipment needed are at our fingertips. If we only take one day a month, that is still one day that sees part of the family's or child's legacy being carefully preserved. If you have never done this before, it is also very enjoyable and relaxing as well. Don't be surprised if the whole family wants to get involved. It's fun, and it's making memories that will last.

The Hope Chest

Chapter Three
The Hidden Gift

Memories

Memories are a hidden treasures stored within our hearts, and often during the hardest times in our lives we dig down and pull those special memories out to help us get through. While we want to create a wonderful physical gift for our daughters through a hope chest, specially created for them through many years and much thought and prayer, it is also important to make sure we are making the "hidden" memories within their hearts that will go with them one day.

The time we take for the little tea parties when they are young, and the effort of reading books aloud that bring enjoyment to all, taking walks in the cool evening together, anything that can become a gift of your time to your daughter can become a treasured memory for her. As mothers, we need to remember to slow down and take the time now while they are still in our arms and our homes. When they are grown we will have plenty of time, but no children to spend it on. The memories of their youth will have been formed, and we will not be able to go back and add to them.

The Hope Chest

Material possessions may be lost, stolen or damaged, but the hidden memories we carry with us are never lost. They are waiting to be used and loved over and over again.

> I learned about *how thieves break through and steal*, and how treasures are better as memories and eternal things rather than gold and material goods. Now we give heirlooms to our children by taking trips together as a family, including aunts and grandmothers and grandfathers as much as possible. Those memories will last even if the pictures we took are destroyed, or their mementos purchased during the trip are lost somehow.
>
> Joan Taylor

There are so many different ways to give our children the gift of our time, and each family and each child in each family will have different areas that are touched with memories. Some of the memories come through the careful planning of events by parents, other memories come from spontaneous moments. Be aware of both kinds of memories and be ready to use them.

Ask your children what their favorite memories are; you might be surprised! It might also give you a glimpse into what they enjoy and help you add memories to the areas that they seem to hold dear to their hearts.

Whether incidents are planned or not, memories happen. How many times through the years have all we all wished we had a camera handy to snap a few pictures of something that had just happened? A little boy catching his first fish and half falling in the water trying to keep it from getting away. Or your daughter stirring strawberry jam on the stove while her nose is stuck in a book. Your little toddler squatting down and pointing a chubby finger at an ant running by. Any mother can think of countless memories in her mind that will be with her forever. If we plan ahead and have a camera handy, these are memories that we can "click and keep." These memories can be passed down to our grandchildren, so they can see their own parents as children, doing many of the same things they too enjoy.

Let's not forget family vacations or family disasters! It's so easy to get busy and forget to take pictures of family members in the midst of enjoying themselves or working together through a crisis.

I have one picture of my mother that I cherish, and it would never have been taken if my brother had not insisted on it. My parents had traveled back to Mother's childhood home for her 25th high school reunion, and my brother and I had been allowed to go along. Mother's home had once consisted of a large cattle ranch that, piece by piece, had been sold off as Grandfather needed the money. Each street had been named after someone in the family, a clause that Grandfather had made when he sold off the land. As we drove through streets and tract homes that were once part of "The Ranch" we came across a street sign that had been put up with my mother's name on it. My brother insisted that mother get out and stand under the street sign and pose for a picture; she was slightly embarrassed but finally agreed. The picture shows my mother with an eternally youthful smile, and it's one of my favorite pictures of her. Six months later she was bedridden with leukemia, and three years later she was gone from our lives. Had my brother not insisted and taken the time for that picture, I would not have such a wonderful memory to hold in my hands and show to my children who never had the chance to meet their grandmother.

Disasters are much the same way, only safety needs to be taken into account when taking the pictures. Is the time it takes to snap the picture going to put anyone or anything in jeopardy? If so, WAIT to take the picture until the timing is more suitable, but still try to get a picture if at all possible. I can think back through the years and remember small and large "disasters" and often I wish I had snapped a picture in the midst of it to remember things. But lost opportunities are truly lost, and I have learned from them.

In 1994 there was an earthquake in Southern California that heavily damaged my sister-in-law's home. Not only was the structure damaged, but the contents inside the house were thrown all over the floors. She literally had to wallow through the muck in her kitchen to begin cleaning up. Peanut butter, honey, olive oil and cornstarch, contents from each and every shelf in her kitchen were sprawled, plastered and dried all over the floor and mixed in with broken and jagged glass. The jagged glass. The dishwasher door had, at some point during the earthquake, bounced open and shut swallowing gulps of items as they fell off the shelves, and the refrigerator doors had been thrown open and closed, tossing out the entire contents to add to what was already piled on the floor. This was only one room of the house.

The earthquake hit at 4:17 am while everyone had been asleep. The large shelving unit at the head of her bed had fallen over on my sister-in law and her husband, trapping them inside. In her son's room, the waterbed mattress had taken flight and landed with a plop and explosion of water onto the floor. The heirloom china and crystal that had been given to her at her wedding, antique china from her grandmother's family, had been shaken out of its cabinet and more than half lay broken at the foot of the stairs. She took pictures both before and after cleaning up the mess. A few weeks after the earthquake she made a picture album, including her own thoughts and memories of the disaster. Newspaper clippings she had saved and her children's memories in their own words were also added to the scrapbook. Now, years later, she and her family occasionally sit and look through the scrapbook, marveling at what they had dealt with and survived. This album is a legacy that she can pass down to her children, grandchildren and great-grandchildren.

All situations, whether good or bad, are memories. Many memories can be retold to children and grandchildren verbally, but there are no physical reminders to add depth and reality to the story. Other memories can be re-told with pictures, clothing or articles to help add detail and depth to the story...the difference between a few minutes of thought, the preparation of having a camera on hand and someone who is willing to keep items for the future.

Inner Knowledge

The girl who has so educated and regulated her intellect, her tastes, her emotions and her moral sense, as to be able to discern the true from the false, will be ready for the faithful performance of whatever work in life is allotted to her; while she who is allowed to grow up ignorant, idle, vain, frivolous, will find herself fitted for no state of existence, and, in after years, with feelings of remorse and despair over a wasted life, may cast reproach upon those in whose trust was reposed her early education.

It is not for women alone that they should seek a higher education of their faculties and powers but for the sake of the communities in which they live, for the sake of the homes in which they rule and govern, and govern immortal souls, and for the sake of those other homes in the humbler walks of life, where they owe duties as ministering spirits as well as in their own, for in proportion as they minister to the comfort and health of others, so do they exalt their own souls.

The Hidden Gift

Women should seek a higher education in order that they may elevate themselves, and that they may prepare themselves for whatever duty they may be called upon to perform. In social life we find that the truest wives, the most patient and careful mothers, the wisest philanthropists and the women of the greatest social influence are women of cultivated minds.

Our Deportment by John Young, 1881

One of the greatest gifts we can give to our children is the inner knowledge they take with them. If I can pass along no other thought in this book, I would like to encourage mothers to teach their daughters the skills that have so often given a new bride the ability to turn her "house" into a "home." Inner knowledge and basic skills are truly the best hope chest a young lady will ever have.

A young bride needs to be able to provide whatever her new family will need, often through the work of her hands. These skills are frowned upon by today's feministic views and materialistic shoppers, but these "hidden skills" are a valuable asset to any hope chest and the future well-being of a family and home.

Becoming a wife and mother was once looked upon as the greatest achievement a female could attain. Staying at home and keeping the household running smoothly, being a help to her husband any way she could, , raising godly children, and being the backbone of the family was what young women were raised to be and do.

> Who can find a virtuous woman? for her price is far above rubies. The heart of her husband doth safely trust in her, so that he shall have no need of spoil. She will do him good and not evil all the days of her life. She seeketh wool, and flax, and worketh willingly with her hands. She is like the merchants' ships; she bringeth her food from afar. She riseth also while it is yet night, and giveth meat to her household, and a portion to her maidens. She considereth a field, and buyeth it; with the fruit of her hands she planteth a vineyard. She girdeth her loins with strength, and strengtheneth her arms. She percieveth that her merchandise is good; her candle goeth not out by night. She layeth her hands to the spindle, and her hands hold the distaff. She stretcheth out her hand to the poor; yea, she reacheth forth her hands to the needy. She is not afraid of the snow for her household; for all her household are clothed with scarlet. She maketh herself coverings of tapestry; her clothing is silk and purple. Her husband is known in the gates, when he sitteth among the elders of the land. She maketh fine linen, and selleth it; and delivereth girdles unto the merchant. Strength and honor are her clothing; and she shall rejoice in time to come. She openeth her mouth with wisdom; and in her tongue is the law of kindness. She looketh well to the ways of her household, and eateth not the bread of idleness. Her children arise up, and call

her blessed; her husband also, and he praiseth her. Many daughters have done virtuously, but thou excellest them all. Favour is deceitful, and beauty is vain: but a woman that feareth the Lord, she shall be praised. Give her the fruit of her hands; and let her own works praise her in the gates.

Proverbs 31:10 -31, KJV

Proverbs 31 speaks about the virtuous woman who has become a godly symbol for many women today. The virtuous woman was a loving wife and mother who was a hard worker and enjoyed the "fruit of her hands." She cared well for her household and reached out to the poor, her husband was respected in the city, not just for his wealth but for the heart of his wife. Her husband and children praised her, she was blessed. This passage speaks again and again of how she "works willingly with her hands." She was always doing something productive, and found enjoyment and delight in her work. In each and every verse she worked with her hands or through her hands. She did not go "to work," but worked through her home and cared for her family, as well as others.

What a wonderful way for the effort of raising godly daughters to be rewarded! To have the work and labor from her OWN hands become a praise to her. What she is able to make or do herself she does not need to purchase or hire others to do. Her hard work pays off not only financially but with respect for her husband, her family and for herself. People trust her, and she is happy with her life.

How true is this of young women today? Have they been taught and encouraged to use their hands industriously, or have they been allowed to sit with idle empty hands, and think only of their own wants and needs? There is a very old saying, "Idle hands aide the devil's work." This is as true today as it was hundreds of years ago. Keep a child busy, and she stays pointed in the right direction and out of trouble.

The Hidden Gift

If you would preserve your children from the pernicious influence of indolence and all its corrupting tendencies, you must be earnest in purpose, active, energetic, and fervent in spirit. Earnestness sharpens the faculties, indolence corrodes and dulls them. By the former we rise higher and higher, by the latter we sink lower and lower. Indolence begets discontent, envy and jealousy, while labor elevates the mind and character. Cultivate in your children habits of thought which will keep their minds occupied upon something that will be of use or advantage, and prevent them from acquiring habits of idleness, if you would secure their future well-being.

It has been said that he who performs no useful act in society, who makes no human being happier, is leading a life of utter selfishness - a life of sin - for a life of selfishness is a life of sin. There is nowhere room for idleness. Work is both a duty and a necessity of our nature, and a befitting reward will ever follow it. To foster and encourage labor in some useful form, is a duty which parents should urge upon their children, if they should seek their best good.

Our Deportment by John Young, 1881

Preparing items for a hope chest is a wonderful way to keep a daughter busy. It helps to teach her the skills she will one day need, and encourage her to "use the skills of her hands to supply the needs of her family," both now and in the future.

The Hope Chest

Many young ladies today do not have the skills that past generations have learned, used and passed on to their children. Today's society could easily be called the "disposable" society. Items are easily gained and easily discarded. There is no pride in a job well-done or a skill learned well. Laziness and instant gratification runs rampant in our young people today. Why should anyone take the time to learn or make something from scratch when they can buy a similar item instantly is the prevailing attitude.

> There is a charm in occupation which can scarcely be understood by idle persons, nor does the enjoyment end when the time has been whiled away; for the permanent results remain in the comfort or gratification we are enabled to give to those around us.

"The Boy Joiner, E. Davidson, 1874

The value of a skill lies in the heart of the person who learns it. Not only is the skill a valuable inner knowledge to have on hand, but it gives an inner pride and feeling of self-worth that can not be found anywhere else. A skill, a knowledge of how to make something well, allows a person to "create." Creating gives a thrill to the heart. Whether the creation is a simple crocheted dishcloth, a musical composition, a poem or beautiful items filling the hope chest...the enjoyment and happiness that fills the heart is the greatest reward.

The Hidden Gift

Once the skill has been learned, the ability to reproduce more for the home, her hope chest or to give as gifts to grandparents or others, allows the child to learn the gift of "giving from the heart," and enables her to enjoy keeping her hands busy. Step by step, block by block, skill by skill until the house is built, and it will be a sturdy house indeed!

Count that day lost whose low-descending sun
Views from thy hand no worthy action done.

The Hope Chest

Chapter Four

Basic Skills

Dreaming dreams of love and honor and usefulness is a pleasant occupation, but making such dreams come true is the worthiest of achievements; and the Hope Chest packed snugly with pretties to wear and useful household necessities is a step in the right direction.

Clothes are the outward sign of attainment, and the home likewise reflects our achievements and proclaims our character and habits as no spoken word possibly can. If the bride-to-be desires to be judged kindly by soon-to-be-acquired relations and new acquaintances, let her look honestly upon herself and her clothes and to the things she prepares for the new home.

A knowledge of sewing is an almost indispensable accomplishment in the home, and no girl can learn how to use the needle more pleasantly than by starting on little pieces of hand embroidery that are soon completed and that possess the charm of beauty as well as the value of usefulness .

The Hope Chest

The desire to create is strong within us all, and an outlet for the expression of ideas and ideals is practically an essential if we are to be truly happy and genuinely useful. Sewing is such an outlet for girls and women.

Poise is the most priceless characteristic a woman can possess, because it makes her mistress of herself and gives her understanding of others. Poise is the serene, steadfast condition of mind that is the result of deep thinking about ourselves, our strength and our weakness. Such thinking is possible only through concentration, and sewing develops concentration, for you can't do fine stitching and let your mind do a one-step.

It is not given to all of us to express ourselves through music, sculpture, drawing, or many other arts or sciences, but women may always express themselves in that wonderful handicraft - needlework. Today, with artistic patterns and designs already stamped on fine materials, and splendid twists and flosses prepared for needlework, there is really no reason why we cannot make this work of our hands an art, and, best of all, an art accessible to all and of a character that everyone who sees can understand and enjoy.

The art of embroidery is centuries old, and marvelous and beautiful are the specimens treasured in museums and art galleries.

Basic Skills

It should be known that to create wonderful things or beautiful things one must first desire to do them and then be able to do them. Ability to do things comes with practice; desire springs from a more subtle source, of which love for and a knowledge of the beautiful in all things and a generous attitude of mind are essential.

Behind everything that is created beautiful, useful or otherwise, there is thought. Thought may be termed the soil of the mind, from which springs inspiration, and these, coupled with concentration and skill, are the forces that create - that develop to completion everything that is made and done.

If we develop these forces as we may, we will do wonderful things, and our lives and the lives of all with whom we come in contact will be better and happier because of our increased power of mind - of our more highly developed skill.

A perfect unison of heart, head and hands is what every woman should strive for. Learning to use the needle skillfully will set you on the right track toward this goal. And in what pleasanter way can women acquire this fine skill of the needle and reap the assured reward than embroidery?

The Hope Chest by H. E. Verran Company, 1917

The Hope Chest

Long accustomed to marrying off daughters, she assembled Catalina's entourage in a business-like manner... Coin, jewels, and plate were packed in substantial leather-covered chests, with Catalina's initials studded in brass nails on their lids... Catalina herself packed her own small personal possessions - her missal, her crucifix, her books and her needlework materials, for her mother had stressed she must continue with her embroidery at which she already showed considerable skill...

Catherine the Queen by Mary M Luke

Here we find a real princess who used her needle with skill and was encouraged by her mother, a queen, to continue with her sewing! Catalina could and would have all she desired at her fingertips, yet she was being encouraged to continue with the simple art of embroidery.

Her mother, no doubt knowing how stressful the life ahead for her daughter would be, knew that simple embroidery would be an easy way for her daughter to relax and be able to think quietly, and at the same time be rewarded by the beautiful items that would come forth through the work and skill of her fingers. There is deep inner reward in doing things with our hands and seeing the effort bear fruit, and this queen and loving mother no doubt knew the benefits of handiwork and passed that wisdom on to her daughter.

Once young women were sought after and judged as

much for their cooking skills and needlework, as for their beauty and grace. A young man looking for a life-long mate would want to know that his wife could care for him and their future children, as well as be an inspiration to him and looked up to by others. Today, many young women enter into marriage with very little knowledge of how to run a home and care for others, because they have "idle hands." This can add undue stress to the new marriage from the start. By allowing your daughter the chance to learn and practice these things in your home, and with your guidance, she should be able to step into her role as wife and mother with a firm foundation beneath her.

> It could only have been an inducement to the young man who was considering a step into matrimony to see such a well-stocked chest in the possession of his intended, and to know that she could sew and embroider so well. For if she took pains with her linen she might be equally assiduous in all her domestic management, darning his socks and cooking his dinner with a proper, craftsmanlike, and wifely devotion.

Love and Courtship in America, 1946

The Hope Chest

Even if a young woman may never have the need to use the skills she has been taught while growing up, they are still there if ever the need arises. Consider it a form of insurance, that will help provide for her future family. The inner knowledge your daughter takes with her could very possibly be the best dowry that she could be given.

> My eldest aunt, now in her early nineties, has quilted for many years. I have a quilt that she made over 30 years ago. It is made with cotton batting that was home-made by her from cotton grown on her own farm, and picked by her hand and my uncle's. Her little living room (and I mean little) was large enough for a quilting frame to hang from the ceiling. She quilted all winter when it was too cold to grow crops and sold the quilts to help make ends meet.
>
> Joan Taylor

We never know when the skills we have learned will be needed to benefit our family or provide food and shelter if our husbands are injured, out of work or die unexpectedly. During the great depression, many people relied on the skills they had learned as children, and they would often barter their services for food, supplies or other goods.

My father would tell us the story of our grandfather who worked in a large factory with a conveyer belt that used a thick leather strap to move it around and around. Every few months the strap would wear thin in places and snap. Grandfather would bring the old strap home and use that to make and repair shoes on a cobbler's bench which he had traded a pig for. His work, though rough and crude, was in big demand for shoe repairs, and he was able to use that skill to help put food on the table for his large family and his in-laws. My father said the leather soles were so thick on the repaired shoes that they would be outgrown before there was hardly any wear to the sole.

My father also told us how his mother would take cabbages grown in their yard and make sauerkraut from them, exchanging this and other produce she had grown for fresh eggs and milk from other neighbors who had chickens and goats. She also took all the old worn clothing, flour sacks and sheets and turned them into usable blanket covers, braided rugs, kitchen towels, baby diapers and patches for clothing. Christmas was entirely hand-made, and we carry this tradition on today in my family. This was improvising and practicality at it's best.

Some of these things may not have been beautiful, but it allowed my father and his family to survive through those depression years until times were better. My father said there was never a time when he and his family were hungry or went without the basic necessities, and they were often able to help neighbors and extended family who were harder hit and unable to make do. Had it not been for the skills his parents had, and the ability to improvise and exchange services with others, the depression years could have easily broken his family apart.

As a result of the depression years, my father gained a great deal of inner knowledge and skill. He served in World War II, and after the war he was able to use his knowledge to build a good life for his wife and family. There were hard times for us as well, but my parents both had that inner knowledge to fall back on, and the ability to improvise through the roughest spots, and we survived with a happy childhood behind us.

The basic skills need to be taught to today's children. God did not create us to be idle and lazy, or to rely on the services and items created by others. Financial stability is never something we can rely on for ourselves, our country or the world. The only thing we can rely on is the inner knowledge and basic skills we have, and the common sense we possess to get us through calamities and hard times. Many will suffer needlessly simply because they have not learned the needed skills, or they thought there was no need to learn them. Others are too proud or too lazy to work with their hands. There is a sense of inner peace knowing you will be able to handle almost anything that comes along because you have that inner knowledge safely tucked away.

The greater the difficulty, the more the glory in surmounting it. Skillful pilots gain their reputation from storms and tempests.

Anonymous

Basic Skills

Though some skills are considered a lost art now, many others have been resurrected and will continue on through the next generation. Following is a list of skills that can be learned and used to add many wonderful items to your daughter's hope chest. Some of these you might not know how to do and may need to learn with your daughter, but there can be a great deal of amusement and delight in mother and daughter learning together. You may surprise yourself by taking up a new hobby, one that will be a blessing to your home, family and yourself.

Thread & Yarn

Basic machine sewing, hand sewing, embroidery, hardanger, crewelry, quilting, cross stitch, mending and darning, crocheting, knitting, spinning, weaving, tatting, smocking, French or heirloom sewing, doll making

Kitchen & Food

Vegetable gardening, canning and drying foods, candy making, cooking and baking: breakfasts - lunches and snacks - main dishes - casseroles - desserts - soups - breads and muffins, cheese making, maple sugaring

Home Skills

Rug braiding, water-color painting, oil painting,

upholstery, basketry and broom making, soap making, candle making, flower arranging, gardening (starting from seed all the way through harvesting and food preservation, trees and berry bushes, flower gardening, herbs, even grains), home management (including finances, care of children and the sick and elderly), raising animals (rabbits can be raised for meat or show in almost any backyard), card making and papermaking, improvising with materials at hand and frugality, keeping family traditions and celebrations, hospitality and caring for others, playing musical instruments, making simple musical instruments, campfire cooking, making and maintaining a fire, cooking with wood, making rope and twine, stenciling, decoupage, flower drying and pressing flowers and uses for both, growing and using gourds, simple games and crafts to keep children entertained, and much, MUCH more…

The test of a classic skill is that it remains eternally modern and useful. The difference between buying or making is the enjoyment and pride we receive in the acquisition and use of the item.

Basic Skills

The Hope Chest

Chapter Five
Music and Religious Education

It is well to remember that every blessing of our lives, every joy of our hearts and every ray of hope shed upon our pathway, have had their origin in religion, and may be traced in all their hallowed, healthful influences to the Bible. With the dawn of childhood, then, in the earliest days of intelligence, should the mind be impressed and stored with religious truth, and nothing should be allowed to exclude or efface it. It should be taught so early that the mind will never remember when it began to learn; it will then have the character of innate, inbred principles, incorporated with their very being.

Our Deportment by John Young, 1881

Never forget that the first book children read is their parents' example - their daily deportment. If this is forgotten you may find, in the loss of your domestic peace, that while your children well know the right path, they follow the wrong.

Childhood is like a mirror, catching and reflecting images all around it. Remember that an impious, profane or vulgar thought may operate upon the heart of a young child like a careless spray of water upon polished steel, staining it with rust that no efforts can thoroughly efface.

Improve the first ten years of life as the golden opportunity, which may never return. It is the seed time, and your harvest depends upon the seed then sown.

Our Deportment by John Young, 1881

Hymns

A "hymn" to many people, is a prayer set to music. If you read the words of those timeless hymns that have stood firm and true, some through hundreds of years, they ARE prayers. Prayers that have stood by countless Christians in good times and bad, through fiery trials, hardships and delights. These prayers are often sent by just a familiar heartfelt melody in our heart, because we are too overwhelmed to think of the words. Yet the melody comes to comfort us, to bring strength to the weary and hope to those lost. They can help us rejoice with those who are happily overflowing and to reach out and encircle those who mourn.

Consider bringing these timeless melodious prayers into your home, and instill them in your children and your children's children. These "musical prayers" are a legacy for every Christian.

Every hymn has a story behind it. Some of their stories are heart wrenching, others filled with praise and joy...but all are awe-inspiring. Our family enjoys learning the history behind the hymns, and it often gives us a greater appreciation for why a hymn was written.

There was a sweet custom at one point in the 1700 - 1800's where the bride and groom would be serenaded by their guests. This was often carried out at the reception while the young couple stood in the middle. The guests encircled the couple holding hands with each person next to them, forming a ring around the newlyweds. Hymns of thankfulness and praise would be sung to the couple, celebrating their new life as husband and wife. Today, this sweet custom has been replaced with popular secular songs and modern dance. Consider bringing this old tradition back into practice and bless the young couple with wonderful memories.

Starting a new family tradition of hymn singing could be a very fun and happy way to make memories and learn the words to the wonderful legacies we have been left. For Christmas, family members could practice singing together several times, and then at some point before Christmas simply record it. By making copies of the tape, you can sneak one into your daughter's hope chest and send extra copies to loved ones far away who will enjoy hearing your little ones' voices sing these precious songs.

Hymn tapes and CD's, either with instrumental music or with singing, are available at all Christian bookstores and internet sites. The hymns can be played throughout the day and will quickly become an integral part of your families life...whether they know it or not!

How To Use Hymns in Your Home

Hymns can be written in beautiful calligraphy and framed for your walls. Calligraphy can become a skill a young lady can learn, either on her own or through classes found at many craft stores. With calligraphy, she can make many beautifully-framed "worded pictures" to place in her hope chest. These pictures could contain many of her favorite Bible verses and hymns. She could also use the skill of calligraphy to create beautiful gifts for others as well. If she ever needs to make a little extra money, she can offer calligraphy services for a fee.

Hymns can be embroidered or cross-stitched and framed as samplers or made into decorative pillows, bookmarks or book covers. There are many counted cross stitch booklets that have beautiful scenes enhancing Bible verses and hymns.

A Theme Quilt can be made using a favorite family hymn. There are quilt blocks that can be embroidered with a hymn or Bible verse which allows your daughter to practice her embroidery skill and also memorize the words. A separate block, with the addition of an embroidered or cross stitched border around the sewn passage, would make a beautiful matching sampler for the quilt.

Your children can practice their handwriting using the words to hymns, and when they have memorized the hymn they can write the words into a special journal. One step more would be to have the child read about the hymn's author, and write a short biography in her special book. This would be a family heirloom for many years.

Old hymn books are often discarded by churches, and they can be easily found even at thrift stores. Look for the ones that have the musical scores inside so your child can play the music. Or the pages of favorite hymns can be carefully removed and professionally mounted and framed for beautiful and inspiring wall pictures.

Some families have purchased a dozen or more of the same old hymnals, usually when churches are discarding them, so they will have plenty on hand for their children and guests to use if there is a "hymn singing."

Group singings are nearly unheard of today, yet they were very common long ago and thoroughly enjoyed by all who attended. Group singings were a time where young people, families or anyone who could attend, gathered together and would have an hour or so of hymn singing. The singing would be followed by a time of socializing and refreshments. It was very popular among the young people especially, because it broke up the dull weekday evenings and allowed them to enjoy fellowship while still being adequately chaperoned.

Traditional group singings were usually on a weekday evening if they were being hosted by an individual or family in their own home. If the singing was being hosted by a church, it was usually on a Friday or Saturday night. Refreshments were always provided, usually by the guests bringing a plate of goodies and the host or hostess providing punch or drinks of some kind.

Some group singings were prearranged, with the hymns already chosen ahead of time. Most were more informal and the hymn suggestions were spontaneous by those present. Personal Bibles and hymnals were brought, unless they were using a church where ample hymnals were readily available. Occasionally there would be a whole day set aside for a singing, usually prior to a large revival meeting, and these were eagerly looked forward to by everyone who lived within walking distance. At these singings, the guests would bring dishes and desserts, and a large pot luck meal would be shared at some point. Today a BBQ or pot luck could be arranged, and if the group is large, a city park could be used as the meeting place. Small and informal, or large and preplanned, this is a wonderful time to get together and enjoy the Lord through singing.

By reviving this old form of entertainment, we can pull our children away from the television at least one night a week, every two weeks, or once a month. It will help them learn and remember the wonderful old hymns, and they can invite their friends and share the Lord with them in an informal way that may bring other young ones to Christ. If families decide to join together and have a night set up every week, every two weeks or once a month, not only the young ones will enjoy getting together, but the parents and even grandparents will look forward to these group singings. Group singings are wonderfully contagious! And you may find that the singing lasts for longer and longer periods as the hymns are learned and requested more often. Don't be surprised if the small group you started out with outgrows your home.

Using both Bible verses and hymns, we can "bring children up in the admonition of the Lord." Music is a very easy and accessible means of instilling the love of God into young hearts. Music is effortless, simply by listening it becomes a part of us. God's laws will be easily written upon our hearts and in a wonderful and enjoyable way.

Let the word of Christ dwell in you richly in all wisdom; teaching and admonishing one another

in psalms and hymns and spiritual songs, singing
with grace in your hearts to the Lord.

Colossians 3: 16, KJV

Something I truly enjoy, is watching children bellowing out hymns in church that they have learned and memorized "most" of the words to. Their little bodies bounce back and forth to the music, their voices sing loudly the parts they know well, and they sing softly or hum the parts that still need to be learned. One of my sons, when he was 18 months old, would "sing" in his jumbled little way along with hymns that he recognized. Even at such a young and tender age he could recognize the music, and he wanted to raise his voice along with all the rest. I have no doubt that Jesus, a lover of children, smiled on this little boy's efforts.

My husband's grandmother, who went home to the Lord in 2001, delighted to tell us one of her fondest childhood memories. She would laugh and giggle over this, and my kids still talk about it even now. When O'ma was 7 years old, she was caught by her Sunday school teacher one day singing "Onward Christians Soldiers," but with a slight and previously unknown twist to the words. The song had been taught earlier that day to the younger Sunday school class, and O'ma had taken it into her little heart and cherished it. O'ma was standing on the old wooden swing behind her house when the Sunday school teacher just happened to pass by and hear the following words bellowing out of the mouth of her tiny pupil for the whole world to hear...

> Onward Christians Soldiers,
> Marching off to war,
> With the cross-eyed Jesus
> Going on before.....

The dear teacher, realizing that her pupil had not quite fully understood the words, very gently explained the difference between "cross of" and "cross-eyed," extracted a promise that the little one would remember the right words, and walked away with a tremendous smile on her face. No doubt she too realized that Jesus would be smiling down on that child's tender heart and not hear the words as much as hear the love that poured out in her voice.

Classical and Other Music

Aside from the valuable loss of hymns in our culture, we have also become a culture that does not spend the time and effort in learning to play musical instruments or to providing wholesome entertainment for our young people.

Once music was considered a blessing in a home, a gift of one's time and energies to bless and entertain others. Today we rely on recorded music. Consider having your children learn to play an instrument; not only does learning to play musical instruments allow a child the knowledge of the great master musicians, but it provides discipline of eyes, hands, mind and timing. It also keeps their minds and hearts pure from the lyrics of today's popular songs, many of which are too profane to even think of, let alone sing along to!

Besides the classical masters of the past, there are wonderful varieties of music that can be enjoyed and collected on tape or CD for your daughter's hope chest: ballads, folk songs, instrumental music, children's songs, Bible passages set to music, seasonal songs like Christmas favorites and more.

Take the time to copy favorite music or songs from one tape to another, or purchase doubles of her favorite music, so she can have it in her home and listen with her children. Music can only be purchased when it is in production and being sold; by the time your daughter is grown with her own children, it may be impossible to find the favorite songs of her youth available for her own children.

So many of my favorite childhood songs, most of which were wonderful Christian children's songs, were all on phonograph records. By the time I was grown, they had not survived through the 5 children in our family. I often wish I still had those songs on tape for my children to enjoy. Now I have copies of my children's favorite tapes to place into their chests for their children to enjoy.

Music and Religious Education

Music as Inner Knowledge

For hundreds of years daughters were taught and encouraged in the art of playing music, whether harp or piano, violin or flute, dulcimer or cello. It was considered a sign of good breeding and was a part of the "gentler arts" of a by-gone era. A short piece played on the piano while entertaining guests or having tea, was considered to be a wonderful form of entertainment. Once more it gave the young lady the ability to use the gift of her hands for the benefit and enjoyment of others.

Learning to play musical instruments can be considered "inner knowledge" that can bless our children in so many ways. It takes real effort on the parents' part to encourage and remind a child to practice day after day. Taking a child to and from music lessons, the cost involved in the lessons, books and the instrument itself...all this lends a ready excuse for many parents to back away from instilling the understanding and basic skill of playing music into their children.

If you are feeling led to give the gift of music to your daughter, whether in the form of recorded tapes or CD's, or by allowing her the opportunity to learn to play an instrument, the Lord will be able bless your efforts one day in the future because you have faithfully laid the groundwork.

Music and Religious Education

The Hope Chest

Chapter Six
Letter Writing

A beautifully hand-written letter is a treasure and well worth keeping. Treasured letters are often found in the oddest places. Stacked, with ribbon wrapped lovingly around them to hold them together, they represent a precious bundle to someone. Many are just run-of-the-mill letters, while others are letters filled with love that the owner could never part with. Even generations later, the ancestors are touched enough to continue preserving them.

> My mother kept many of her mother's letters, as she had married and moved away. When my grandmother passed away, my mother lovingly wrapped up all the letters she had saved over the past couple of years before Grandmother's death, with dried roses from her coffin top and lovely silk ribbons. You see this type of thing in magazines, but this was a stack of love next to her bedside, until one day, an avalanche hit their home while they were away. Snow was in that bedroom and the letters had six feet of snow on top of them. My husband and I had to

take care of the details while they were gone and the "only" thing that they both made mention of to retrieve if possible were the stack of letters and my grandparents' special Bible. That's it! Nothing else mattered.

My dear husband and I broke away the wet wall next to this room as we had access to it through a room barely filled with snow and it was partly in a stairwell. We felt like treasure hunters using tools to claw the wet gyproc off, sift through the glass-ridden snow, digging like mad (I was five months pregnant !) and tried to keep everything safe within that situation. After several hours of digging....there they were under a squished night table...soaking wet! We took them home, laid them all over the carpet next to heaters to dry them up and almost 30% of them had no writing left....the ink got wet and disappeared. My mother cried over this loss....she missed her mother so much and it had not yet even been a year since she had wrapped them up.

Renee Blokzyl

Letter Writing

Letter writing was once an art that young ladies were taught and expected to use. Correspondence was dutifully carried out each week or even daily in some instances. As much effort went into the actual writing of the letter, making each and every stroke of the pen as beautifully as possible, as did the effort of the wording itself. The Spenserian handwriting that took years to master has been lost, and now we struggle through quickly scrawled notes hastily written down with no thought of the poor person who will be forced to read them!

> There were old chests in the attic, too, which were full of papers and letters. The letters include Civil-War period letters from wives to their husbands who were off fighting. Those are treasures, to be sure. The beautiful, old-style handwriting of this particular young woman (who addressed her husband as "Mr. Shaw" on paper), is an artwork in itself.
>
> Joan Taylor

Whether we are writing a grocery list or a love letter, does our penmanship matter? Yes, it does. The character of the person shows in her writing, whether the writing is the mundane grocery list or whether it is a letter to a lifelong beloved friend. Beautiful writing becomes a habit as easily as bad, illegible writing does. Taking the time to teach our children to write with nice, legible writing adds a grace and beauty to their character. It shows with each stroke of the pen that your child has discipline of mind and hand, and care is being taken about what the final result will look like. There is never a lazy, illegible word to be seen; even in haste beauty is found.

This is an important aspect in today's society of computers, email and cell phones. It is not often that we are called on to actually "hand-write" anything anymore, and the skill is being lost. Although most people who see beautiful writing appreciate it, and often wish they could write so well, there is no push for today's children to learn and practice this skill.

Teach your children while they are first learning to write how to work diligently for a beautiful result. Put effort into the process, and your children will have beautiful handwriting that will be appreciated by everyone they come in contact with. If your children have already formed their handwriting habits, it's never too late to improve them. I have a child who learned many of her numbers and letters backwards. With a lot of practice, she has learned how to write them the correct way. Practice and learning is not always easy and can be very time-consuming for parents. Children also get bored easily with repetition.

There are many ways to overcome these problems. The use of pretty paper can make the entire process something special and encourage children to put extra effort into their writing practice. Using old-fashioned inkwells and pen and nibs for writing is something every child will enjoy...I guarantee it. My children honestly cannot get enough of this! The actual "scratching" of the writing nib on paper is a tactile learning method and is rewarding because the child can hear, feel and see the results. The ink comes in a rainbow of colors, and some are even scented now. There are also gold and silver metallic inks that glimmer and shine as well, so there is a very wide variety to choose from. The nibs come in all widths and sizes, and writing this way easily leads into calligraphy, which is another wonderful skill to add to your child's "inner knowledge" area.

Children can send off a letter each week to someone they care about; a grandmother or another relative would be happy to receive little notes. Is there someone who needs a note to cheer them up? Has anyone done something for your family that the children can thank with a hand-written note? Pen-pals are another option for letter writing as well.

Keeping and preserving letters, notes and cards that someone has blessed you with can be a living treasure. I have sent and received letters that have been saved and re-read over and over again. The words contained inside can often be timeless, and though written for one person, have meaning and strength for others too. Encouraging your daughter to start and maintain a scrapbook of letters, notes or cards that have been sent to her personally or to the family as a whole, can be a blessing years from now. She can read through it and remember the people and the reason for the written letters in her book.

Saving letters can also be a way to look back and see your personal growth over many years. The writings of a young child are centered around what is important to them in their little world; the people and pets and daily activities show through in their words. Teenagers will talk about themselves and what they like or dislike and the dreams they have. A young wife and mother will have a vastly different perspective only years after those teenage dreams, and the reality of life is often harsh but refreshing to see in someone who is just starting to experience it. A mother with nearly grown children will have gained a great deal through the struggles of raising children and being a wife, and she will have great insight to give to others. A woman whose children are all grown and married will be able to look back and see what was truly important in those years, and she can bless others if they listen. An elderly lady has many memories that should be written down and saved and usually has an inner peace in her life as she looks forward to shortly walking with the Lord. Your daughter may one day need these letters to fall on during hard times and struggles, and she will have them at her fingertips if she has taken the time and effort to save them. Children would be able to gain from the insight left by a great-grandmother they had never seen, simply because someone saved a letter.

Handwriting and the ability to write beautiful "written" letters, in comparison to email and computer-

Letter Writing

-ized letters, is indeed an inner knowledge that can bless our children. Included in each of my daughter's hope chests will be a wooden lap-top writing desk. It will be complete with pens and nibs, a variety of ink bottles tucked neatly inside, and a large amount of stationary for letter writing. It is my hope that not only will the words they use, but the beautiful writing itself, bless someone who least expects it.

The Hope Chest

Chapter Seven
Journal Keeping

I use the term "journal keeping" instead of "diary" for a reason. A diary often leaves the impression of a self-centered kind of written record. A journal is simply a written record of a journey. *Life* is a journey. Living a Christian life is an incredible journey. So keeping a journal as opposed to a diary allows us to write what is happening to us at any given time. We can record the results of prayer, obedience and our growing love for Christ while working through life and all the wonders and hardships it presents to us. It is all written down in our own hand, to go over and remind us of how often He has blessed us, held us, and gifted us unexpectedly. Our life, carefully and honestly recorded, can benefit us with an outlet for our thoughts and emotions. Years later it can be a wonderful treasury of insight, showing how our physical and spiritual lives have intermeshed.

Each person will have different times when they feel the need to write in their journal. Some may feel they need to record their thoughts and experiences on a daily basis, others a weekly or monthly basis, and still others when they feel led. There is no right or wrong way to keep a journal, it is a personal path of communicating with ourselves and our Father.

My children are given a very special journal when they receive their hope chests. By the age of twelve or thirteen, they will have already started along the "journey" of their lives. At this age, it is easier for them to record their thoughts and their heart than it would be if they were younger. For the first year they are required to spend at least one hour a week thinking, if not writing, about the "journey" they are on. In this way, it lays a foundation for them to continue on their own. Each parent will have different thoughts on this topic, and a different way to meet the end result.

It is never too late to start your own journal if you have not started one already. Use your quiet time with the Lord to jot down what you feel led to write, what verses He has placed on your heart or what struggles you are going through. In many ways the thinking, prayer and writing help us sort out and deal with our problems and allow us to enjoy and save our happiness.

The time I have found to be most beneficial and peaceful is late at night when my husband and children are sleeping and the house is quiet for the first time that day. This is when I am awake and feel drawn to Him by the utter silence in our home. I have tried to get up early in the morning as others often suggest, but that is just not the time for me. My mind is centered on the day ahead and what needs to be done around the house

Journal Keeping

I start to wonder when my children will wake up and worry that I will have to end my time of intercession earlier than I would like. And often I am just too tired to get up! In other words I am too easily distracted to be able to spend quality time with Him in the early morn. But late at night, when I am awake already and the day is done, when peace has flooded my home and I am able to say "Thank you Lord"...that is when He draws me in and holds me close.

Types of Journals

A journal is the written record of a journey. *Any* journey. It is up to the writer of the journal to decide, at some point, that there is a need to purchase a journal and spend the time writing in one.

The most commonly known journal would be the "diary." There are many others however. Bible journals are common, where the writer records what she has learned and experienced through her Bible reading and study. Nature journals record observations, provide a place for documentation and learning experiences, as well as areas for specimen samples and hand drawn or painted pictures of items.

> One of the things I cherish is my grandmother's 10th grade botany notebook (1925?) It is full of her sketches and notes and also has pressed flowers and leaves on nearly every page. I found it

after she died. Always knew we shared a love for flowers, so this is a meaningful thing for me to have.

Mona

There are school journals, music journals, story journals for writers, family history journals, family read-aloud journals (to list all the books and reviews from the family's read-aloud time), sewing journals, friendship journals, courtship and wedding journals, vacation journals and any kind of journal someone feels led to start.

We encourage our girls to keep a special journal during their time of getting to know their future husband through courtship. This will become a special keepsake I am sure.

Pam True

Journal keeping is a wonderful way for us to learn and to practice handwriting. It also allows us to think deeply, and to consider and form written words before putting them down on paper. Although journal keeping is most often used as a personal investment of time and energy, and for the enjoyment and ability to look back and refresh our memories, it can also unknowingly be a blessing to others.

One caution when keeping a journal, especially a courtship journal, would be to keep it honest without over-doing the emotional aspect. Thoughts that are put in writing can often come back to haunt us when we least expect it. Nothing should ever be written out that we would be ashamed for others to read. Although we may be a little embarrassed to have another person gaze upon sentimental words, it is far better to be embarrassed than ashamed of what we have written about others or ourselves. Being sentimental or honest is one thing. Being emotional and stating things that no one else should hear or read is quite another. This is a good rule to follow whether we are writing in a personal journal, or sending a love letter to our betrothed.

The Love Letter:

Of this it may be only said, that while it may be expressive of sincere esteem and affection, it should be of a dignified tone, and written in such a style, that if it should ever come under the eyes of others than the party to whom it was written, there may be found in it nothing of which the writer may be ashamed, either of silliness or of extravagant expression."

Our Deportment by John Young, 1881

The Hope Chest

Chapter Eight
Single Daughters

As mothers, we want only the very best for our daughters. But what the best is in our own eyes may not be what the Lord has planned. We have our own dreams of how our dear sweet girl will become engaged to a wonderful man, the beautiful wedding and a happy marriage for her blessed with children. This is normal for parents to expect and to plan and prepare for. Yet, what is the Lord calling your daughter to do and be, and what is His timing for her future life?

I believe in courtship and witnessed it firsthand in the church I grew up in as a child. No dating, only courtship. This was long before it was fashionable in Christian and homeschooling circles. It was something awesome to witness, it was pure and sweet and honorable before God.

Courtship and marriage were not even considered until the young adults were fully mature and felt the Lord calling them to be married. When they felt that calling, they would go to the elders of the church and pray with them, for the Lord to bring them a spouse.

And then they waited. This was not something parents went out and tried to accomplish on behalf of their children. This was a covenant between the young adults and the Lord.

Some waited many years before a spouse was brought before them by the Lord. During that time, they grew stronger in faith and found a deeper love for Christ. Their life continued, with college and jobs, while they waited for marriage. It is much better to be single, than to jump into a hasty marriage and be miserable or divorce years later. God's timing and His ways are perfect...it is our human-ness that refuses to wait.

These young people would often be the helping hands that fellow church members needed. Elderly people were driven to doctor's appointments, young mothers were given relief for several hours while young people watched their children, home repairs were quickly done with groups of the young men working together, meals were brought to those who were ill or injured, homes were cleaned when there was a need for it. When there was a need, the young people would step in, and they became an extension of God's love. Through their hands and efforts, God was able to bless those He loved and those who needed help.

Some of these young adults had a spouse brought before them quickly, and the Lord blessed them with marriage. Others waited for years, and the Lord never sent them a spouse. They did not become bitter, or anxious, but turned their hearts to God and became an extension of His love to all those around them. They were blessings to others, and few people can imagine how special those fellow brothers and sisters were. They were not living for themselves, but for Christ, and it showed in their love for their fellow man.

There are many passages in the Bible that speak of being single.

> But I would have you without carefulness. He that is unmarried careth for the things that belong to the Lord, how he may please the Lord: But he that is married careth for the things that are of the world, how he may please his wife. There is a difference also between a wife and a virgin. The unmarried woman careth for the things of the Lord, that she may be holy both in body and in spirit: but she that is married careth for the things of the world, how she may please her husband.
>
> 1 Corinthians 7: 32 - 34, KJV

A single woman was once considered to be an embarrassment to the family. She was called a spinster, an old maid, an unwanted woman, a woman not worthy to be a man's wife. Yet in many ways this "unwanted woman" was a silent, quiet blessing to many around her. She was nurse when her family and neighbors were sick, she cared for her siblings' families, she tutored children, she worked for the church in untold and countless ways, she was a blessing for her parents when they were old and feeble. There is no embarrassment in these tasks; in many ways they are the Lord's hands at work.

Many of the missionaries that have gone to foreign countries were able to go because they were single and needed to care and worry only for themselves and the Lord's work. These missionaries, both male and female, were mightily used by God to bring so many lost souls into His flock. Gladys Alyward, Amy Carmichael, Florence Nightingale, Clara Barton, Betty Greene, Lottie Moon, Mother Teresa, Corrie ten Boom are just a few of these godly single women. The deeds they were able to accomplish for His good are more than most of us could ever dream of. These young women were called by Him for His purpose, though many of them had family that thought otherwise. If they had been restrained and urged into marriage, instead of following His call, many countless souls would have been lost. The young women themselves would no doubt have carried throughout their life the question of whether they had done the right thing. What an incredible burden to carry, or to force onto another.

It is one thing for us to hope, pray and plan for our daughters to marry and begin a new life, but we also need to be aware that there will be some who are called to a different purpose and a different life. We need to be willing to let go of our dreams and selfish wants and allow His leading in our children's lives.

We are placed on this earth for one purpose, and one purpose only. That is to serve God all the days of our lives. Some will be called to serve through marriage and the raising of the next generation and others through being single and available for His use. Yes, children are to respect their parents and try to follow their wishes, but the Bible warns us not to put other wants or desires over what God is asking of us. As parents we need to watch and pray and see if the Lord has chosen our daughters for marriage or for being single and respond appropriately. This is very hard for some parents, and I have witnessed firsthand how these parents can force their daughter to choose a life or husband she felt was wrong for her. Heartache followed. Parents who urge their daughter to choose marriage, when she is not being called at that time to marry, are going against the Lord and His will.

Never give up hope, and continue to pray that the Lord will bless your daughter with marriage and a happy home, if that is where your heart is. She may be halfway through her life before the Lord brings a husband to her, but that union will be blessed by Him, and she will have been able to serve the Lord in the interim in ways we may never know. We have no idea how many ways the Lord can use a heart completely open and focused on Him.

> Our Lord does not call women to preach, but He surely commands them as well as men, "Go work in My vineyard.
>
> Lottie Moon - Missionary

How true she was! And how much we need to listen! For those unfamiliar with Lottie Moon, she and her sister Edmonia were missionaries in the northern provinve of Shantung, China. Although Edmonia's health deteriorated and she was forced to go back to the United States, Lottie continued on with the mission's work.

Before Lottie became a missionary to China, she had been a schoolteacher in Virginia. The first thing she did when she reached China was to open a school for girls. This was a struggle from the beginning since Chinese culture believed the most important part of being a female was to have feet properly bound, to get married, and to do the mundane tasks that were too lowly for men to perform.

After the school opened and Lottie began teaching she was exposed firsthand to the painful process of foot binding. She determined that the horrible and painful tradition would change. Twenty-five years later the Heavenly Foot Society was known throughout China and was supported by Chinese Christians and others who helped put an end to foot binding in China. Lottie Moon was a small woman with a great faith in God. She was able to change China's inhumane tradition and spread God's word in a very special way.

One young woman can make an incredible difference if the Lord calls her and she is able to follow. Lottie Moon is only one example out of thousands. Florence Nightingale changed the medical profession and set high standards that saved hundreds of thousands of lives, and her ideals still continue to be used today. Amy Carmichael was a wonder in herself, to endure such suffering and be such a beacon of God's love shining through her and drawing so many to Him. Thousands of motherless children felt her loving touch.

Is this not what we should be praying for, for our children? That the Lord would be able to use them in whatever way He sees best? Whether as wives and mothers or as His helpers, and for us to be thankful in whatever His decision is? This may be a call for us to give a great sacrifice of our wants and wishes, yet if He has asked it of us, should we not consent willingly and be thankful that He has found in our daughters a vessel for His usefulness?

I bring all this before my readers as food for thought; it may be that several of you will have daughters who will be the next Gladys Alyward, Lottie Moon or Amy Carmichael. For the mother of the daughter who marries, this small amount of writing, I hope, will have left you with an understanding how single daughters are a blessing too. A mother should not judge, or feel her daughter is superior to another young lady simply because she has married. Very few young ladies will be called to live a different and unique life for God's glory, and they should be praised and loved for it. Our goal should be to teach and train our children so that when they are grown the Lord can use them the best way He sees fit. Marriage or otherwise, it is truly ALL in His very capable hands.

How does all this tie in with hope chests? A daughter, whether married or not, will always be blessed by what has been put aside for her and by the skills and knowledge that she has been taught through the years of her childhood. Memories of wonderful times shared with her family and friends are easily taken with her wherever she goes.

Do not assume that an unmarried daughter will have no need of a hope chest, or that the time and effort you put into helping her create a beautiful hope chest was all in vain. It isn't! She will cherish it just as much if not more than a married daughter would, and parents should take pride in having created a beautiful and timeless gift.

The inner knowledge that she has learned and been able to practice and experience at home, will be a wonderful "physical" inheritance for her. The ability and willingness to use her hands to bless others will also enable her to spread the love of God in silent subtle ways that speak more than a thousand words could ever tell.

Your efforts in creating a hope chest for your daughter will always be a special treasure for her. The idea behind the hope chest is the most important thing to remember. The love, hope and dreams parents have for their daughter are shown in a very special and physical way with each and every item they have searched for, considered and either accepted or declined. The hope chest is for blessing your daughter in her future life, whatever future that is, and only God knows that.

The Hope Chest

Chapter Nine
Sons

A family with sons should not miss the wonderful opportunity to place aside special items and mementos of their sons' youth. The same ideas and ideals in this book can also be geared towards your sons. Don't miss the opportunity to give a blessing to your son as well as your daughter.

Your son may or may not be interested in what his parents are saving for him, but this should not be a discouragement to you. Keep saving and place old toys, drawn pictures, favorite books and what-nots into a cardboard box or container.

Along with each item you may want to include a little note with the date, the history behind the object and why it has been saved. Remember that you and your son can always throw things away later, but it is impossible to go back and retrieve things once they have been discarded!

My husband's only childhood treasure is a small cigar box, filled with bits and pieces of his Boy Scout days. He does not have a baby photo of himself or any other trinkets from his childhood. It's just assumed that don't need or want these things, so very little, if anything, is kept for them. Although it is not something that my husband dwells on, he does enjoy coming across that old beat-up cigar box when we clean out the closet. Many times he has pulled something out of the box and told our children about the time he earned this or that Boy Scout medal or badge. The children have "ooohhhhed" and "aaahhhed" over them. It brings a smile to his face every time. If you were to ask him whether he wanted to keep those trinkets he would tell you to go ahead and throw them away, that he doesn't need them. But I've seen his smiles, and I know better. So the cigar box and its hidden trinkets will always find a safe place to hide until the next time we come across them...if only to see him smile once more.

My brother on the other hand, has many items from his childhood that he cherishes. He has kept his treasures in an army foot locker that was given to him as a teenager. Among his most treasured possessions in that chest are our parents' Bibles.

Men may differ in their ideas about what is important to them, but they will enjoy and be thankful for the effort it takes to set aside special items that were important to them as children and even as adults. My husband is still amazed that I have saved so many things from his career in my hope chest. He was pleasantly surprised to come across several items while we went through my hope chest to write this book. The small amount of effort I went to, to make sure the papers, pictures and other items actually made it safely inside my hope chest has paid off and will one day be handed down to our children.

I would encourage all parents to make a concerted effort to put aside special items for their sons as well as their daughters. Even if your son is not impressed, his future bride will be thrilled!

A young bride can't help but enjoy the gift of a chest full of her husbands' childhood treasures, all neatly saved and packed away by his parents for the day he married. What a wonderful surprise to be able to sit down and go through it with her new husband! How fun it would be to hear the memories attached to each article and to hold the same things her husband once held dear to his heart and played with as a child.

Family heirlooms passed down to a son and daughter-in-law to start their new life would be a wonderful surprise for any bride and one that she would hold dear to her heart. This is a wonderful way for a new daughter-in-law to be welcomed into the family and know that plans were in place for her happiness long before a face appeared for their son to marry.

With a little forethought and effort, your grandchildren will be blessed to play with the same things your son played with in his youth, and they will have many wonderful treasures to go through with their father, all neatly packed away in his chest waiting to be explored.

My sons will each take with them a complete toolbox. The information they will need to use the tools and make home repairs will be something they have learned and practiced at home. This, to me, is a gift that many young men lack in today's society. They need to know simple car repair, simple carpentry skills and home repair, appliance repair, etc. A toolbox full of tools he has learned to use through the years, ready whenever he will have need for them, is a gift that will go a long way to provide for your son's future family.

As your son grows older, you may want to encourage him to make a hope chest for his future bride and store all the treasures you have saved for him safely inside. A son will never be too tough or grown up to enjoy trinkets from his past. There is still a little boy in every grown man.

Sons

The Hope Chest

Chapter Ten
Brothers & Sisters

A brother can be such a trial to a sister, especially when they are close in age! Brothers and sisters are each other's best friends and worst enemies, and they teach each other how to love and care for one another by trial and error. What brother does not like to see his sister happy? What brother does not have moments and thoughts of wanting to do something special for his sister...in between fits of annoying and antagonizing her? What brother does not try to comfort a crying sister, often crying along with her when her heart is truly broken? The bond between a brother and sister can be very strong, lasting a lifetime.

A hope chest created with hard work and given in love, from a brother to a sister, will have far-reaching memories. A handmade quilt from a sister to her brother would be equally special. Both can become a link that will be a reminder for each sibling after they are grown and far away from each other. It is a "physical tie" that binds two hearts together.

Whether a brother is led to make a hope chest for his sister out of a sense of duty or love, or because it is something required of him, it is still a wonderful opportunity for him to not only work with his hands for the benefit of others, but to pass on to to his sister something very special.

A brother can help his father build a hope chest for his sister, or if the father has passed away or left the family, take over the whole task. A son with a disabled father could be a blessing if the two were able to work together to create a special hope chest. Today there are many different lifestyles and reasons why a father may not be able to build a hope chest for his daughter, but there is no reason why a brother can not fill this role and create a special heirloom for his sister.

If help is needed there are church members, family members, neighbors and even college courses that can help with the construction and use of tools and wood. A young man only needs to ask to receive help, and in many ways, it blesses the person who is able to help the young man as well.

With a simple design and some very basic tools, anyone can build a hope chest, even mothers! The important thing is to remember to start out simple and build on experience. It is very natural to want to make a beautifully exquisite hope chest, but quite another thing to carry those plans through to completion! Start small and build on that, one step at a time.

A young man may also want to make a chest for his future bride, his mother if she does not have one, multiple sisters, female cousins or nieces, his grandmother or anyone else he feels would enjoy and be blessed by one. There is no reason to stop at hope chests either, but to continue with recipe boxes, jewelry boxes, writing desks, cradles and even hand-carved items like candlesticks and wooden toys. The possibilities are endless...and he may find that he enjoys using his hands and creating items that bring pleasure to others. What a blessing! What a lifelong legacy to work with!

A brother can be a very important person in a young lady's life. He is her protector when her parents are busy elsewhere. He is her helper when she is not able do something alone. He is her friend and confidant on important matters, and her conspirator on others. The relationship between a brother and sister is uniquely special, as is the bond of love between them.

On the other hand, let's not overlook the influence a sister, either younger or older, has on her brother. She helps curb his rough edges, she is light where he is heavy, her tongue can have a sting when he needs to be restrained from wrongdoing, she comforts his heart when mother is not available...sisters are dear to their brothers, whether the brother openly admits it or not. A mother helps to form the character of her son, a sister often defines that character through play and daily living.

The Hope Chest

Girls, and especially those who are members of large families, have much influence at home, where brothers delight in their sisters, and where parents look fondly down on their dear daughters, and pray that their example may influence the boys for good. Girls have much in their power with regard to those boys; they have it in their power to make them gentler, purer, truer, to give them higher opinions of women; to soften their manners and ways; to tone down rough places, and shape sharp, angular corners.

All this, to be done well, must be done by imperceptibly influencing them, and giving them an example of the gentleness, the purity, the politeness and tenderness we wish them to emulate. When we see boys careless with their elders, rude in manner and coarse in speech, and we know that they have sisters, we often, and I think with reason, conclude that there must be something wrong, and that the sisters are not trying to make them better boys, but leaving things alone, letting them go their own course. Perhaps their excuse would be that they were too much occupied themselves and that their own studies and pursuits prevent them from being able to pay much attention to their brothers; and "boys will be boys," you know. By all means let boys be boys. I, for one, regard boys far to highly to wish them to be otherwise; but the roughness, and coarseness, and rudeness, of which I speak, are necessary ingredients of boyhood; and it is you, their sisters, who must prove that they are not. Interest yourselves in their pursuits, show them, by every means in your power, that you do not consider them and their doings beneath your notice; spare an hour from your practicing, from your drawing, from your languages, for their boating or sports, and don't turn contemptuously away from the books and amusements in which they delight, as if, though good enough for them, they are immeasurably below you. Try this behavior, girls, for a short time; it will not harm you, and you will benefit them greatly. You will soon find how a gentle word will turn off a sharp answer; how a grieved look will effectually reprove an unfitting expression; how gratefully a small kindness will be received; and how unbounded will be the power for good you will obtain by a continuance of this conduct.

Equally great will a girl's influence be on her young sisters, in whose eyes she is the perfection of grace and goodness, in whose thoughts she is ever present. Beautiful, exceedingly beautiful, is the close friendship between an elder and a younger sister; but let the elder beware of the influence she exerts. If she herself be careless, frivolous, undutiful, and irreligious, the child will inevitably be so too, unless the fatal influence be counteracted by some other holier one. If she gives sharp answers, or shows but little regard for truth, let her not be astonished if the little one be ill-tempered and untruthful; and sorrowful will be the conviction that she has had not a little to do with making her so.

The Hope Chest

"We know not half the power for good or ill,
Our daily lives possess o'er one another;
A careless word may help a soul to kill,
Or by one look we may redeem our brother.

'Tis not the great things that we do or say,
But idle words forget as soon as spoken;
And little, thoughtless deeds of every day
Are stumbling blocks on which the weak are broken."

Anonymous, 1878

Brothers & Sisters

The Hope Chest

Chapter Eleven
Mother's Own Chest

Although this book has been written with the daughter in mind, a mother has every reason and right to have a hope chest of her own...even though she is married with older children or is even a grandmother!

It's never too late to start your own hope chest. Instead of making and setting aside items for your wedding, you will be storing memories of your married life and the husband and children that you have been blessed with.

Into this chest should go all the treasures that everyday life hands to you, as well as the special ones from vacations and family celebrations. Everything that you can and will be setting aside for your daughter's chest can also be put into yours, such as the little papers and special items the children make, remembrances of family times, pictures and scrap albums. Make one for your daughter and one for you. There are usually more than enough items to go around, and instead of throwing them all away, take the time to put them in a safe place.

This will be a special treat you can share with your grandchildren when they come to visit. Should anything ever happen to your daughter's hope chest and the items inside, whether fire, theft, flood or otherwise, you will have a back-up to share with her.

You can also be setting aside special things for your grandchildren that can be given to them later as their wedding gifts: quilts you have made for each one, baby items, family history set down on paper, anything that touches your heart and you feel would be a blessing to pass on to the future great-grandchildren can be safely stored within your chest. As a precaution, always pin or somehow attach a note on each article telling whom the item is for and the date and the history or reason behind it. You want to take the time, now, to make sure it will get into the right hands should anything ever happen to you.

A Simple Warning

There is only one caution that should be taken in the accumulation of items for the hope chest as well as the chest itself, and this should be taken to heart by each of us and shared with our daughters.

A hope chest is a beautiful and very special gift that should be cherished, and it is given and received in love. But it should never become such an important part of our lives that it becomes an idol and stands between us and God. With each and every item I place inside, I pray that it will be used to bless my daughter and that it will never become an idol to her or a stumbling block for what is important in life. It is there to enrich and expand her life, not to cause her to become a slave to it or to become a burden for her to carry or care for.

Anything can easily become an idol, no matter how seemingly innocent it may be. My mother struggled with the baby books she had so carefully created for each of her children. They were very dear to her heart and something that was irreplaceable to her. Footprints, locks of hair, photos, first baby words, all the weight and height information on a growing child, records for the first five years of each child's life...everything was carefully written down and saved. Eventually her spiritual struggle became so strong that she had to choose between the books and the Lord. She destroyed the books. It was not an easy thing for her to do, but she did that rather than lose her dearest Friend. I was 6 at the time, and it is still an incredible lesson for me to this day.

I believe it pleases God when we are happy with what He has given us. I think He knows some things will become quite dear to our hearts too. This undoubtedly is pleasing to Him, because we carefully tend to what He has placed in our hands. Yet He is unwilling to share that deeper part of our hearts, reserved only for what are the most important things to us...our God first and our family second. Material possessions have no place here.

God gives us so many gifts, many of which we take

for granted daily and others that we begin to place on pedestals. There should be a balance between our thankfulness and joy in our treasures and the ability to turn away from them if needed. God, as any father, enjoys making His children happy and providing for them. But when the gifts stand in the way between Father and child, this creates a real problem. We need to be responsible with our hearts and minds and constantly remember what is the most important thing in our lives ...our Heavenly Father.

> Lay not up for yourselves treasures upon the earth, where moth and rust doth corrupt, and where thieves break through and steal: But lay up for yourselves treasures in heaven, where neither moth nor rust corrupt, and where thieves do not break through and steal: For where your treasure is, there will your heart be also.
>
> Matthew 6: 19 - 21, KJV

We need to remember and instill in our daughters that the real treasures are the memories we carry with us, the inner knowledge that we have learned through our lives, and most importantly our walk with the Lord. Everything that comes after this, including a beautifully made and carefully thought-out and prepared hope chest, simply emphasizes the real treasures.

Mother's Own Chest

Never Too Late for a Hope Chest

It is never too late to begin a hope chest for some-one. Whether your daughter is a child, teenager, a young lady out on her own or still at home, or if she is married with children, a hope chest is a lovely gift at any time. If Mother, Grandmother or Great-Grandmother has never enjoyed a hope chest, it's time to bless them with one.

Just by starting today, and placing special items aside, you are creating a hope chest. Your hope chest may start out as a shoebox and grow into a larger, room-ier box. You may suddenly come across a hope chest or blanket chest in an antique or thrift store and find you have a gleam in your eye and a silly smile on your face when you realize what you could do with that old chest. You may ask your husband or son to make you a chest for your birthday or Christmas, or just to make one NOW.

If you have lived this long without a hope chest, there is absolutely no reason why you can't have one now. They are a special link to your past, your future, and something you will treasure through the years ahead.

Here are a few suggestions to get you started, but the best suggestion, of course, is to "just start!"

The Hope Chest

Teenage Daughters

If a daughter is in her late teens, there is still plenty of time to start creating a hope chest for her. There is also time to help her learn the different skills that will enable her to add items to her hope chest. The feeling of pride and accomplishment is far greater in the hand-made items she will be able to make and set aside than anything she will be able to purchase in the future. The encouragement in the use of her hands while in her teens can reward her throughout her life. With both mother and daughter working together, the amount and quality of the articles will grow quickly and be a beautiful start to her new home.

If there are very few mementos from her childhood that have been saved, take the time to make memories of the friends she has now and the things she is interested in. Pictures of events, special teas with a new tea-cup to save and put away, projects that your daughter has done either alone or with friends, pieces of her schoolwork she put a great deal of effort into, fabric saved from her clothing to make a quilt for her or her children, even buttons from special dresses can be used on infant clothing for her future babies.

Look at your daughter, really look at her and watch her. Find her interests and pay attention to what is important to her. Try to save or collect those memories for her. What may be important to you may not be to your daughter, so try to see where her interests are and go from there.

Grown or Married Daughters

If your daughter is completely grown, whether she is married yet or not, you can still create special gifts and find unique items to place inside a chest and surprise your daughter.

Choose special things you have saved through the years she will be happy to see again. Pictures and papers placed into a scrap book, items you have bought or made yourself or a single cup and saucer from a set you have owned and used through her childhood would all be very simple little things and inexpensive too. A very special item could be a scrapbook you have carefully made, writing down as many memories as you can about your daughter and the family, in your own handwriting. This might be time-consuming, but I can't think of a single person who would not be utterly thrilled to have such a special book created just for her. And what a legacy would be waiting for your grandchildren through that simple little book!

Even if you have saved nothing at all, or it has all been lost in some way, you still have the ability to share the love you have for your daughter in many ways through the items that you can make or purchase especially for her. Place baby items inside the chest for her firstborn or her 14th child! Find special articles that you know will bless her each and every time she sees or uses them. You can even save items that can be kept in the hope chest for your grandchildren when they are grown. The possibilities are endless with thought and prayer.

Whether you present her with the chest on a special day, or maybe when she is struggling through hard times, or just out of the blue...it will be a very special memory for all of you to share.

Once she has her hope chest, she will begin adding to it herself. You can still present her with your love offerings from time to time, and she will be very thankful you were thinking of her. The hope chest and the items inside may not be in your home any longer, but it is still a link between your heart and hers.

Granddaughters

Your daughter has her hope chest. It was filled, and she is married now with children of her own. Maybe she is very busy and just can't seem to find the time to devote to preparing a hope chest for her daughter. Or perhaps she would like to start on the project and would like you to help. Or maybe she has even started but can't seem to find the time to continue or has run out of ideas. Or your grandchildren need help learning to use their hands productively, and you have a skill they can learn. There are many ways that a grandmother can continue to bless her own daughter and begin to bless her granddaughters with the hope chest in mind!

Before you begin, take time to think and pray about what your role will be in your granddaughter's hope chest. This is so important. Perhaps you should make items and save them without letting your daughter and grandchildren know, so that they can be blessed with a wonderful surprise from you one day. Or it could be that your daughter wants to create a hope chest for each child and would be offended if you were to "take over" and do it yourself. Taking time to consider everyone's roles in the project and where you will be useful will allow your efforts to be a help, and you can avoid interfering or offending anyone.

There is one dear elderly widow I know, who is in poor health, with arthritis in her hands and feet. This wonderful little lady has a hard time using her hands or walking, but it is her wish to keep her hands busy. She has always had something in her hands to do or work on, and she simply can't sit still without "doing" something with her hands. Needlework is too hard for her eyes, and she has trouble holding a needle due to the arthritis, but crocheting and knitting are skills she is able to accomplish in short spurts.

A few years ago, she decided that she would crochet or knit a special item for each of her grandchildren, some who are still infants themselves. These items will be safely tucked away by the grandchildren's mothers for the day they are married, to be given as a wedding gift from a grandmother who will not be there to witness their joy. Each of these items will be handknit or crocheted, and every inch of yarn or thread will have passed through the loving hands of Grandmother. Grandmother will never see the beautiful little newborns that will someday wear the tiny sweaters, hats and booties she has made, or see the beautiful young faces of her grandson's brides wrapped up snug and warm in the afghans she is making for them, but the desire to provide for future happiness is, in itself, love made visible.

Mothers and Grandmothers

Have you always longed for a hope chest, but have never been gifted with one? It's never too late to make one for yourself. Instead of preparing for marriage, you would be collecting the memories of your life and accumulating a vast treasury to pass on to your loved ones. There is no reason why a mother or grandmother cannot begin, at *any* age, to work on her hope chest. The treasures you keep and set aside in your chest will allow future children in your family to know and understand who you were and what you held dear to your heart. In many ways it will become your "legacy of love" that will be passed down to future little souls who would never have had the opportunity to have known you any other way.

Mother's Own Chest

The Hope Chest

Chapter Twelve
Showers

There are many kinds of showers, but the most popular of all is that given to the engaged girl. Friends are never so good-naturedly generous as when a young woman confides that she has given her heart in love. The bridal shower is a pleasant and sensible way for friends and acquaintances to present gifts that would seem too trifling if they were presented singly. The custom has an interesting background, and it's origin takes us across the sea to Holland.

Many, many years ago - so the tradition runs - a beautiful young Dutch maiden gave her heart to the village miller who was so good to the poor and the needy that he himself had but few worldly goods. He gave his bread and flour free to those who could not pay, and because of his goodness everyone loved him. Everyone but the girl's father. She must not marry him, he said. She must marry the man he had selected - a fat, horrid, wealthy man with a farm and a hundred pigs! - or she would lose her dowry.

The Hope Chest

The miller was sad, and the girl wept on his shoulder. The people who had eaten of the good miller's bread were sad, too. Couldn't something be done about it? Couldn't they give the girl a dowry so that she could marry their kind miller and make him happy? They didn't have much money, it is true, but each one thought of a gift that he or she could contribute.

And they came to the girl in a gay procession: one with an old Dutch vase; one with some fine blue plates for the kitchen shelf; one with strong linens made on the hand looms at home; one with a great shiny pot. They showered her with gifts and gave her a finer dowry than ever her father could! There was a solemn wedding ceremony and jolly wedding feast, and even the father came at last to wish them happiness.

A good many years later, an Englishwoman heard of a friend who was about to be married and decided that the only gift she could afford was too slight an expression of her good wishes. Remembering the story of the Dutch "shower" and knowing that there were other friends who felt precisely as she did, she called them together and suggested that they present their gifts all at the same time. The "shower" that they gave was so successful that fashionable society adopted the custom, and it has remained ever since.

The New Book of Etiquette, 1924

Showers

A shower for the bride-to-be can truly be a blessing if it is done properly and with forethought and effort on the part of the hostess. This should be a time for blessing the new bride with items she will need and not for showing off in any way or hoping for expensive gift items. Practicality and frugality should hold an honored place at these showers.

There are many different theme showers that can be given for the bride-to-be. It would be wise to spread these out somewhat so they continue to be a fun time for the friends and relatives of the bride. If you choose to host several kinds of showers, they should be informal and fun. Having a potluck meal get-together is a wonderful idea, and it helps keep the cost of the multiple showers low. Another shower can have an "afternoon tea" theme to it, with everyone bringing their own cup and saucer. Yet another shower can be a "board or card game" theme, where everyone brings chips, dip, and drinks and plays games. Leave room open for these smaller informal showers where very inexpensive and small gift items are given to the bride.

If you would like to have one formal bridal shower, by all means do so. There should be a formal bridal shower, and it should be as special as you can make it. This shower will be the "big" sendoff for your daughter from all those who love her.

The person for whom the shower is being given should not suspect, as that would spoil the fun. She should be invited simply "to tea" and her invitation should be for an hour later than the time set for the other guests to arrive. No elaborate decoration is necessary, nor is it advisable to plan any sort of entertainment, for the chief entertainment of the afternoon is the opening by the bride-elect of one package after another, disclosing the gifts and thanking the donors.

The New Book of Etiquette, 1924

It was once tradition to give several kinds of showers, each one with a specific purpose in mind. Today we have lost the wonderful ideals and purpose behind the showers, and it has turned into one large frivolous party. Showers today have no real meaning except to follow the newer modern version where everything is combined into one large shower and high-priced gifts are presented to the bride-to-be, often selected from the bridal registry list.

Included here are many wonderful ideas for informal fun showers, or you can invent your own. These showers should be fun, with no emphasis placed on perfection or the quantity of the gifts. That is secondary to the enjoyment and time together for the bride-to-be and her guests. There is no reason why the traditional showers should not be brought back for your daughter and her guests to enjoy. By spreading them out over several months, it will be something that everyone can look forward to. And she will be able to accumulate many small items needed for her new home without causing financial stress on her friends and family.

The Favorite Recipe Shower

A "favorite recipe" shower is a fun way to provide refreshments for the shower, with each guest bringing a dish and the recipe for it. The hostess arranges beforehand for each guest to bring her best or favorite recipe which is written on a pretty recipe card and signed and dated by the giver. The recipe cards can be individual ones from each guest, or the hostess can present each guest with a special card that will match all the other recipe cards. If matching cards are chosen, consider sending the card with the invitation, so the guest has plenty of time to write down the recipe. If a guest is unable to attend, she also has the option of sending the recipe card back to the hostess to be included in the recipe file. This is a wonderful way to include family and friends who live too far away to attend the shower.

Each recipe should be placed under the right heading in a special recipe box and then presented by the hostess to guest of honor. It is usually the privilege of the hostess to provide and prepare the recipe cards and recipe box. If the hostess prefers a notebook to recipe cards, she should find one that is spiral bound and try to arrange a time for the guests to write their recipes down prior to the shower. This may not always be feasible, so recipe cards are usually the preferred choice.

Another twist to the recipe shower is to have each

guest choose a recipe that can be made from "stored food." Items like canned goods, dried goods and possibly frozen goods would be part of the recipe. The guests should bring the recipe as well as all the food items needed to the party, to help stock the bride-to-be's new pantry.

As a hostess, it may be a good idea to have extra recipe cards and pens on hand, just in case you have guests who would like to copy a recipe for dishes they have enjoyed eating at the shower.

The Linen Shower

At a linen shower, any item considered to be "linen" or made from fabric is an appropriate gift. Some of the more traditional gifts were often marked or monogrammed bath towels, hand towels and wash cloths. Other items were quilts, blankets, sheets, embroidered pillowcases, dresser or table scarves, doilies, a tea cozy, tablecloths, napkins, kitchen towels, hot pads, dish cloths, aprons and more.

If a "towel shower" is given, and if the hostess can take the time to arrange it, a whole set of bath towels can be purchased, one or two pieces by each guest, and all monogrammed with the brides' initials. If the bride-to-be already has a set of towels, perhaps a "sheet shower" or one with another theme can be given for something that she could use.

If there is someone who is handy with embroidery,

or has an embroidery machine, and she would like to offer to embroider a few or even all the linens as her special gift to the bride-to-be, this will allow all the gifts from the shower to match in their monogramming style. But this will need to be done ahead of time. If there is no one available who is handy with a needle, for an additional charge some stores will have the items monogrammed for you, or you can find small business that will also do this for a fee.

A Friendship Quilt can be made ahead of time, with the hostess overseeing the making of it and obtaining clothing samples from the different guests. The clothing would be made into a beautiful quilt to grace the bridal bed. Or, if each guest were to bring a special quilt block made specifically for the bride, each block signed by the maker, these could be sewn together to make a quilt top. Perhaps another shower could be arranged for all the guests to help hand-quilt the top or tie it down.

Consider what linen or fabric items the new bride will need, and center a shower around those needs. If you are unsure what her needs are, *please* ask her! A gift and a shower are always welcome, but to end up with doubles or even triples of items that a bride already has, and to have items that are really not needed, is something of a waste. This is not unusual either; many brides end up with doubles or triples, and they often unable to return them all. So don't be shy...ask!

The Hope Chest

The Kitchen Shower

Long ago the kitchen shower was to entertain the bride as well as help provide her with the basic necessities for a kitchen. A hostess who knows the needs of the bride-to-be and can help supervise the guests, by giving suggestions on needed items, will be a very welcome blessing. This helps avoid an over-abundance of any one item, like the egg beater, measuring spoons or hot pads.

Have a simple list of inexpensive items that the bride can use, and send a copy of the list in the shower invitation to the guests. As the guests RSVP for the shower, you can check off the items that have been purchased by each guest. This will allow the guests to give items that the bride-to-be specifically needs, like measuring spoons and cups, pot or pan and strainer, without giving extras or unneeded items.

The kitchen shower should be for the smaller items the bride-to-be will need and not place an un-necessary burden on any of the guests to provide something expensive. Cooking spoons and utensils, salt and pepper shakers, common spices in jars, egg slicers, spatulas, a metal whisk, hot pads for the tabletop, placemats, paper towel holder, small kitchen scale, can opener, bottle cap opener, graters, biscuit cutters, cookie cutters, potato peeler, oven thermometer, candy thermometer, flour sifter, potato masher, pastry blender, rolling pin, cooling

racks, kitchen clock, kitchen timer and other small inexpensive items are appropriate for this shower.

The emphasis should be the enjoyment of all present, and the gifts a token of the affection each guest
has for the bride-to-be. Everyone can afford one of
these little gadgets, so there is no worry that someone
will not be able to attend due to the financial cost of a
gift. If a pot luck meal is provided, this is a fun and easy
get-together that will help defray the cost for the young
bride after the wedding.

The Pantry Shower

For this shower, the hostess has planned a wonderful form of entertainment. Perhaps a high tea is
planned, or a night of playing board games, or watching
a special rental movie or another type of entertainment.

The invitation would have asked the guests to bring
several items they think would be a welcome gift for
the bride's new pantry. This helps defray the cost of
buying starter items for her new kitchen. Some examples would be: baking powder, baking soda, salt, pepper,
sugar, brown sugar, powdered sugar, food coloring,
flour, assorted spices, vanilla extract, canned fruit,
canned vegetables, canned meat, dried beans or noodles,
canned sauces, salad dressing, mayonnaise, oil, vinegar,
salsa, bread crumbs, tea bags, coffee, powdered creamer,
etc.

Other items might include paper items: papertowels,

muffin cups, napkins, paper plates, plastic utensils, paper cups, tissue boxes, even toilet paper!

The Glass, Steel, Aluminum or 'Other' Shower

These showers are centered around one specific material. Glass bowls, vases, drinking glasses, wine glasses, platters, casserole dishes, mixing cups or bowls are only a few items in the glass category.

Stainless steel pots, serving spoons, frying pans, spatulas, mixing bowls, measuring cups, teaspoons, aluminum bread pans, muffin pans, cake pans, cookie sheets, cooling racks and more would be in the metal category.

"Other" can include anything like a roasting pan, tea kettle, coffee pot, stock pots, canners, or many other items. Grannyware, which is the speckled enamel coated metal, is often a good alternative to the high-priced "pure" steel or aluminum items.

Categories of the different items can be determined and suggestions written down. Again, the cost should not be burden to any guest, so make sure there are enough low-priced items.

Other categories for similar showers could be:

Paper - envelopes, stationary, assortment of cards, stapler, scotch tape dispenser, waste basket, calendar, address book, assorted paper clips and other similar items and more.

Laundry Supplies - iron, ironing board, spray bottles, laundry soap, stain remover, laundry baskets, drying rack, lingerie bag.

Plants - either artificial silk plants or flower displays, or real houseplants to be given right before the wedding to make the new home beautiful.

Entertainment - Board games, cards, movies, CD's, music, etc.

Tools - assorted tools for the bride-to-be's small under-the-sink tool chest, smoke alarms, fire extinguishers, emergency candles or lanterns, and other useful "new home" items.

First Aid and Herbal Kits - to stock the new home with needed items, make sure you ask the bride what items she would appreciate receiving and if there are any allergies to medications or herbal treatments that should be avoided.

The Book Shower

For this shower, anything can be included from the Bible to the current best-seller. The hostess of the shower can supply a bookcase as her gift, or if she likes, an attractive book rack or shelf, while the guests supply the books. Again, the hostess would be wise in having the invited guests let her know which book is being given to avoid duplicates. And each guest should inscribe a note inside the cover of the book she gives, and her name and the date.

The Apron Shower

A young lady who enjoys pretty things will enjoy having an apron shower. The gifts could include dainty tea aprons, substantial kitchen aprons, canning aprons, roomy sewing aprons with a sewn in pincushion, great white cooking aprons, baby-bathing aprons (for the future), gardening aprons, BBQ aprons and any others you can think of. Create a shower game, inviting the guests to come up with unique apron ideas and uses. All the aprons the bride receives can be packed neatly into a crisp new laundry bag for the bride to carry home.

The Picture Shower

The picture shower puts happiness into every room. Just a few close friends are invited, and each one brings a framed picture for a room in the new house: one for the dining room, one for the living room, one for the bedroom, one for the hall. The wise hostess will see that notes are exchanged beforehand so that none of the pictures are duplicated and there is sufficient variety to appeal to the bride. No one should attempt a picture shower who is not familiar with the taste of the person for whom the pictures are intended.

The New Book of Etiquette, 1924

If there is uncertainty about what pictures the bride would enjoy, it would be best to instead have the guests bring a nice frame. What new bride can not use picture frames for all those wedding photos? The gift of a mirror or two would not be unwelcome either.

Comfort or Miscellaneous Showers

The idea behind the comfort shower was to provide items for the bride-to-be that were not necessary but would make her home more comfortable. Pillows with removable and washable slip covers, small slumber or throw pillows, monogrammed laundry bags instead of a laundry hamper, colored throw blankets, flannel covers for hot water bottles, hand-embroidered or hand decorated book covers, reading lamps, small throw rugs or anything that would add to the comfort and happiness of the bride and her new home could be included at the comfort shower.

The comfort shower began in the very early 1900's, and it appears that through the years many of these old theme showers were combined together, to produce the "everything-in-one" showers that are given today.

Suggestions for Hosting a Shower

Bridal showers are usually given on weekends in the afternoon, and if they do not include a luncheon, some kind of refreshment is usually served. Consider making it easy and fun by having a shower where a potluck, barbeque, pizza delivery, submarine sandwiches, dip' n' chip, veggies n' dip, homemade ice cream and cookies, or a tea party can be used as the refreshments.

If the bride is working, and is not able to free her weekends for a shower, or a surprise shower is planned, an evening shower is an easy alternative. You can also have a shower following a church service on Sunday if that will work out for everyone.

You may also want to consider having a shower as part of a "high tea" entertainment. Here is a wonderful explanation of what "high tea" is, by a lovely lady who teaches this lost art to young children today:

> Traditional high tea or afternoon tea was (is) served between 4 and 6 PM. Anna the 7th, Duchess of Bedford is believed to have been the originator of "afternoon tea" which she had sent with "tray of sandwiches, cakes and tea" to her boudoir. A little later on, this type of afternoon tea was then enjoyed in the drawing room...it soon be-

came a time for social visits. This became a British National habit, still very popular today.

In our present day, "high tea" has been popping up all over North America. Each year sees the opening of new "tea houses" which specialize in high tea for their customers' afternoon enjoyment. Not just enjoyed between 4 and 6, but any time of day now. There is as much pleasure in the surroundings, the tea and sandwiches and sweets, cream scones with clotted cream (heavy cream in England or whip cream here) and jam...usually served on tiered trays. This is the time to be properly attired (dresses or skirts for ladies), minding your manners and appreciating the genre which includes music to elevate the spirit. A time for peace and pleasant conversation.

This memory maker can be enjoyed to celebrate a birthday, an engagement, a wedding or baby shower, a baptism or just the sheer pleasure of enjoying afternoon tea with family or friends. I highly recommend mother and daughter, grandmother and granddaughter taking high tea together. When and where to have high tea? It can be anywhere...your home, a tea house, your friend's home or if you wish to go uptown, the Ritz!"

Faye Filiatrault

The Hope Chest

Groom's Shower - No Stags Allowed!

There is one more "shower" that you might like to consider. That is a shower for the groom! Granted, the term "shower" might be a tad unmanly, so the host or hostess can rename this little get-together if they wish. Instead of having a stag party, or something similar, consider hosting a barbeque, pizza or submarine sandwich "groom shower."

There are three types of acceptable showers for young Christian men. One is the light-hearted, joke-filled, fun night that he spends with his close friends, who bestow on him silly and useless gifts for his amusement. This is harmless fun at its best, and a good stress reliever right before the wedding!

The second type of shower is the more formal shower, dedicated to preparing the young man for his new career as a husband. This too can be a very fun and happy time for the young husband-to-be and his friends and family members. But the gifts will be items that he will need and use. The host can furnish a large metal tool chest, and each guest can bring a tool gift to fill the chest. The tool shower is the most commonly heard-of and often very appreciated if the groom has never "physically" prepared himself to be a husband and future father. Tools are something almost every man on earth can use or would like to have handy. Other ideas

Showers

could be how-to books, automotive supplies and tools, yard tools and any other ideas "the men" might have.

Showers for grooms appear to be very popular at this writing, though they are more generally silly and humorous in character than otherwise. Instead of a shower of pleasant gifts, the groom is usually greeted with a non-too-gentle barrage of packages containing such ridiculous gifts as gaudy socks meant for display rather than wear, bow ties eight inches wide, lace-trimmed handkerchiefs, a budget book, an alarm clock, a curling iron. These gifts are usually wrapped in yards and yards of paper that must be patiently unwound by the groom. And tucked in with them are bits of written advice and suggestions that cause as much merriment as the gift themselves.

But there is no reason why a young man's friends may not shower him with gifts if they feel that he would welcome and appreciate such an expression of friendliness from them. Most men would feel sheepish at receiving ties and socks and handkerchiefs in a "bridal shower" from friends, but the same men would appreciate a book shower, for instance, or a shower of smoking necessities.

When a shower is given for a man, the women arrange the tea or luncheon, providing the place and the eatables, and the men supply the gifts.

The New Book of Etiquette, 1924

The Hope Chest

The third type of shower is a little more detailed and complex. This would be given directly before the wedding, when the bride and groom have picked out where they will be living. The "shower" would be time donated to helping prepare the apartment or house for the young couple. Guests could give gifts of their time, either a few hours, an afternoon or a whole day. They would be helping the groom with cleaning and painting the walls and floors, checking and fixing the plumbing in the bathroom and kitchen, checking appliances and all outlets in the new home, moving the heavy items into the new home, putting up shelves and pictures where they are wanted, helping with any yard work or cleaning out a messy garage and generally trying to be a help wherever they are needed.

If the young couple has bought a house that is a fixer-upper, it would be a wonderful gift to have help fixing the basics around the house. Patching the roof if it leaks, laying new carpet or flooring, installing new toilets or sinks or tubs, replacing any broken windows, installing new appliances if necessary, trimming over-grown trees and shrubs in the yard, and anything else that would take a great deal of effort if the new husband was working alone, would be appreciated.

Once all the heavy things have been handled, then the bride could have a day where her friends and family come to help her set up her new home. Dishes could be put away, linens stored, the bathroom and kitchen disinfected, windows scrubbed and left spotless and shiny, curtains hung, rugs laid out. A place for everything, and everything in its place... the little home is set and ready for the new couple, all they need now is God's blessing.

A Happy Home Defined

Six things are requisite to create a happy home. Integrity must be the architect, and tidiness the upholsterer. It must be warmed by affection, and lightened up with cheerfulness, and industry must be the ventilator, renewing the atmosphere and bringing in fresh salubrity day by day; while over all, as a protecting canopy and glory, nothing will suffice except the blessings of God."

Rev. Dr. Hamilton, 1878

The Hope Chest

Chapter Thirteen
Trousseau

The word "trousseau" is from *trusse*, which means a little bundle. It is easy to understand how long ago a young bride would take the few garments she owned, tie them up in a little bundle and carry them off to her new home. The average wardrobe would consist of two to three dresses, a nightgown or two, knit stockings, petticoats or other undergarments and a pair of shoes.

If the young lady's family was prosperous, wealthy or part of royalty, of course the amounts of clothing she would be taking with her would reflect those circumstances. But for the peasant or working-class family, clothing and shoes were a luxury.

> The mediaeval trousseaux were rich and elaborate. The royal trousseau of Isabella of France, who was married in 1308 to Edward II, suggests the general trend of that time. An eyewitness records Isabella's trousseau and reports that the trousseaux of lesser brides were only less elaborate.

> She [Isabella] brought two gold crowns

The Hope Chest

ornamented with gems, gold and silver drinking vessels, golden spoons and fifty silver plates. Her dresses were made of gold and silver stuff, velvet and taffetas. She had six dresses of green cloth, six of rose scarlet and many costly furs. For linen she had 419 yards, and the tapestries for her chamber were elaborate with the arms of England and France woven in gold.

Catherine the Queen by Mary M Luke

Following are several quotes taken from old book sources; they may give you a glimpse into what was once considered appropriate to have for a trousseau. Obviously times have changed since these were written, but there is still a great deal of insight and practicality hidden in these words. Just modernize some of the choices, and you have a ready-made list of trousseau items for your daughter.

A sensible trousseau for the bride who expects to travel a little before settling into the routine of housekeeping, who expects to visit interesting places where good clothes are essential for peace of mind and pride of appearance, includes such items as we list here:

◊ At least one custom-tailored or tailor-made suit with an appropriate hat
◊ Several pretty blouses suitable to be worn with this suit
◊ A top-coat or wrap
◊ An evening wrap

Trousseau

◊ Two or three afternoon dresses
◊ Three dinner dresses suitable also for semi-formal evening occasions
◊ At least two evening dresses
◊ One or two pretty tea gowns
◊ Hats appropriate for these gowns
◊ Shoes suitable for walking, for evening wear, and for use with afternoon and dinner dresses
◊ Six pairs of short gloves and three to six pairs of long gloves
◊ One to two dozen pairs of stockings, including those for evening use and sport use
◊ Sweater and skirt outfits for use in the country
◊ Handkerchiefs and other accessories

To this one adds an appropriate costume for golf if one is to play golf, a tennis dress if one is to play tennis, a swimming suit if one is to swim. The personal trousseau depends entirely, of course, upon whether one is going to Palm Beach by steamer or Alaska by airplane, whether one is going to be in Bermuda for just a week or in Europe for several months. A sage rule is to buy only what you know you will need; anything else can be purchased later if needed.

Underclothes are no longer selected for durability but for beauty. The bride wants the frilliest, daintiest chemises and negligees she can find. The average trousseau includes at least one bathrobe, two negligees, six to twelve chemises, six to twelve under sets, six to twelve nightgowns, three breakfast coats, and one or two boudoir jackets. A pair of mules and a pair of bedroom slippers are generally included.

The New Etiquette, 1924

The Hope Chest

Many articles of women's apparel are not seriously affected at any time by fashion changes, and it is not only possible but advisable to prepare such garments early for the trousseau. If time is plentiful, they can be made more cheaply and more beautifully with hand-trimming that will outwear any manufactured trimming that can be purchased; besides, they will have an intrinsic value that cannot be disputed. If the right material is used such garments can be handed on from one generation to another with pardonable pride.

Strive to procure good fabrics, so that the finished garment will be all that it should be. For an adequate and altogether satisfactory supply of undergarments the quantity of lingerie listed here should be sufficient for one year. Few brides prepare for a longer period.

6 nightdresses
6 combinations
6 brassieres or corset covers
4 petticoats
2 dressing sacques
2 negligees

1 Bridal Set consisting of:
1 nightdress
1 combination
1 brassiere
1 petticoat
1 dressing sacque
1 negligee

Trousseau

The bridal set may be made of finer material than that used for the regulation garments, and all the pieces of the set should be trimmed with the same grade and design of embroidery or lace.

The Hope Chest by H. E. Verran, 1917

Initials and Monograms:

All the garments mentioned may be hand embroidered, the bridal set, of course, more elaborately than the other pieces; or, if other trimming, such as lace or machine embroidery, is preferred for some of the pieces, do not fail to mark each piece with an embroidered initial or monogram done in white.

And do you know that all the clothing, as well as the household linen prepared before the marriage, should be marked with the girl's initials? (Author's note: This was to show that in no way was the bride "kept" by her future husband. That she was not a "bought woman". It was also customary that the engaged woman not accept any kind of wearing apparel from her fiancée as that would give the appearance that he is "keeping her." Accessories like a shawl, sweater, or hat were acceptable, but a dress or shoes were not. Appearances were important long ago and should be as well today.) An initial or monogram not larger than three-fourths inch is suitable for all lingerie pieces except the petticoat, which may have a one or one-half inch marking placed just

just above the ruffle on the left side front.

It is not considered good taste to use colored floss for such markings, except possibly when a colored voile or batiste is used. To be quite correct any color that is used should be delicate in tint.

If the combinations or the nightdresses are made with a yoke, place the initial or the monogram on the center front or on the left side front; if the garment has no yoke place it about two and one-half inches from the neck line.

On dressing sacques and negligees place the monogram same as on night dresses, or on the left sleeve, or on a pocket or collar.

If petticoats or negligees are made of silk or satin, or if the negligees are made of challis, flannel or crepe, solid floss should be employed for decorations and markings.

Other Clothes Requisites:

A dozen or more good linen handkerchiefs, each having an initial or monogram marked with floss, may be completed without difficulty, and, if you want to make handkerchiefs with hand-hemstitched hems the same floss is what you will need.

Dainty handkerchiefs done in delicate colors of embroidery floss make a pretty addition to the supply of handkerchiefs.

Trousseau

Aprons for afternoons may be done in white or in colors, the size and number of the floss that is best to use depending on the material and the character of the design. Bear in mind that the proper size of floss is one of the points on which hinges the beauty of the finished article.

Then there are blouses and dresses to be made, on which a little well-applied needlework done with the correct floss in harmonizing colors, or in white, will be a most appropriate and modish trimming. Boudoir caps may be embroidered, also cases and bags for wearing apparel and toilet requisites. These should be marked with an initial or monogram even if they are otherwise decorated with hand work.

Crocheted lace is most attractive and serviceable for lingerie, especially yokes for nightdresses and combinations; but you don't want to put time and energy into such work unless you are sure that the thread you employ is perfect and durable. For the lace edges and yokes you may use pure white or colors."

The Hope Chest by H. E. Verran, 1917

The Hope Chest

Although the clothing mentioned may be outdated for today's brides, it is still interesting to see that the bride at the turn of the century still had thoughts and needs for her future as a new wife. As well as a dowry or hope chest that was set up with the new home in mind, preparing for her future life and children, the trousseau has a similar purpose. The trousseau provides clothing for the new wife so that there will be no need to purchase any items for several years to come.

You may not be able to afford an entire wardrobe for your daughter, or even wish to send one with her when she marries. She may already have ample clothing to last for many years. However, if you do decide to include a wardrobe, or update part of her wardrobe, carefully consider the basic necessities first. These will be what she will have on hand for many years to come, and they should be good quality, long lasting, easy to wash and care for and interchangeable for more options in style and dress.

Nightgowns or pajamas do not go out of style and can be made or bought long in advance and neatly wrapped and tucked inside the chest. Undergarments, socks and stockings, slippers and a sturdy warm coat or jacket are also items that retain their style and usefulness. Your daughter may already have plenty of these that she can take with her, or she may need to have newer ones purchased before her wedding. A coat or jacket, bought in a classic style, can be worn for many years, even when the fashionable ones have come and gone.

A bridal set could be a special gift and could be made ahead of time, or over several years. Elaborate embroidery or heirloom sewing could be used in its creation, or a very plain set embellished with only a colored ribbon would be a sweet look as well. French or heirloom sewing, smocking, lavish embroidery and hand-crocheted lace or tatted lace can be slowly accomplished as time permits and turned into a very special set for your daughter's wedding night. If care is taken with these items, she will one day be able to give them to her daughter as well.

Today the trousseau is nearly extinct, and what most people think of when they hear the word "trousseau" is the cheap, frilly, sexual lingerie that can be found in nearly any department store. From the quotes previously mentioned, we see the "original beginnings" of the trousseau were practical, everyday wearable clothing, and not just the frilly night clothes of today. The thought in mind for both the hope chest and trousseau should be to provide the young bride with items she will need and use in her new home, and to allow the young couple to start their new life without the financial burden of purchasing everything they need at the beginning. A traditional trousseau walks hand in hand with the hope chest to fulfill this need.

The Hope Chest

Chapter Fourteen
Gifts From the Bride

It was once a common tradition for the bride and groom to give gifts to their attendants and even to the wedding guests themselves. The wealthy could afford to shower upon their guests' heads pieces of silver or gold coins or jewels. For the less wealthy, pieces of the wedding cake would be boxed and sent home with the guests.

Today we have had the misfortune to step away from those traditions, and seldom are gifts given to the attendants. Those who are fortunate to have a gift bestowed upon them are usually given identical items purchased for all the attendants.

Instead, consider an individual gift, handmade or specifically searched for and chosen, to be a precious reminder of the special day both the giver and receiver shared. It does not need to be elaborate but something that has heart-strings attached. A small sachet cross-stitched by the bride, a new or antique locket with the attendant's and bride's photos inside, a special teacup and saucer...there are endless ideas, and each gift can be tailor made for each attendant. Such a special and unique gift will have unforgettable memories attached to it. Each time the attendant views or uses the item, it will bring back many happy thoughts and memories for her. Isn't this worth a little extra effort on the part of the bride?

Upon those who attend her at her marriage, the bride is expected to bestow some gift as a memento of the happy occasion. Such gifts vary in character according to the financial standing of the bride and her personal feelings. They can be almost anything she chooses to give.

What more fitting gift can a happy bride-to-be give her attendants than some article for their Hope Chest? And something that is the result of her skill with the needle should possess a value far in excess of a purchased article.

A useful piece of linen marked with an initial or a monogram, a pretty needlework apron, a bewitching boudoir cap, a dressing sacque - all these are the things that not only will delight for the moment, but will recall happy remembrances every time the article is used in after life.

A girl of very moderate means can make such gifts for very little money, because fine new things are always being put out in such variety as to make a happy choice possible.

The Hope Chest by H. E. Verran, 1917

Gifts From the Bride

This embroidery pattern, as well as the patterns in the back of this book, are original French Monogram patterns from 1880. A very nice monogram initial alphabet can be found on page 377 for your enjoyment and embroidery practice. The above full-size pattern may also be used, as well as any other patterns you find throughout the pages of this book.

The initials are centered and nestled into the design. For a wedding gift, usually the groom's initials or first name initial will be on the left side and the bride's on the right. Or, you can use these patterns for an individual person and put the first, middle and last initials in the center.

Hope Chest Legacy offers the complete set of French Embroidery patterns at: www.HopeChestLegacy.com.

The Hope Chest

Chapter Fifteen
Preparing the Items
and
Packing the Chest

You have taken the time and effort to search out or make by hand each item for the hope chest. What do you do with them now, and how do you pack the chest? Every effort should be made to safeguard the items against any damage once they are in the hope chest or stored in boxes.

There are several points that should be made before we progress to actually preparing and packing the items themselves.

First, anything that goes into the chest has the potential to affect all the other items as well, especially moisture! Moisture is a destroyer of heirlooms in the form of molds and mildews. Every precaution should be taken to avoid allowing moisture inside the hope chest. As an added precaution, moisture absorbers can be placed inside the chest, but should be changed frequently. This depends on what you have placed inside the chest and where you live.

Linens should be freshly washed and carefully dried prior to placing inside. Any dirty fabric has the potential to be a breeder of odors, molds and bacteria that can affect any and all other items in the hope chest. Caution beforehand can prevent a disaster in the form of mold and odors spreading throughout the chest. Dirty fabric can also draw insects and cause damage by the bugs eating your treasures for lunch. No matter how clean it looks, unless it has been washed and *thoroughly* dried, do not place it inside the hope chest. It is not worth the risk when you take the entire chest's contents into perspective against just one possibly dirty item.

If you are unable to wash the item when you first find or make it, place it in a box or paper bag until there is time to launder it properly. Do not place it in a plastic bag, especially if you seal the item inside. This allows moisture and bacteria to congeal and the mold to spread very quickly. Even with a tiny food spot or other dirty areas that are on the item, the spot can often contain a very small amount of moisture. If you were to close the item up and seal it inside of a plastic bag, this would allow moisture to form inside the plastic bag in a sweat, adding direct moisture back to the item. This closed environment, complete with small amounts of moisture, bacteria and a food medium make the perfect incubator for quick mold and mildew growth. A few precautions can be the difference between preventing a disaster or discarding a loved and treasured item that has been consumed by mold.

Moisture is the first concern, and odors are the second. All items should be as free from odors as possible, and anything that is questionable you may want to place in a box and set in a closet to prevent the odor from permeating the entire contents of the hope chest.

Books often have an old dusty, musty or smoky smell. If this is a problem for you, you may want to air them prior to placing them in the hope chest. If airing the book for several weeks does not help, try placing it into a plastic bag, with a smaller plastic bag holding a fabric softener sheet inside. Leave the small bag open, and close the larger bag around the book and the small bag. This allows the dryer sheet to impregnate the air in the bag with its perfumed odor and force the odor into the book, but it does not let the oils from the dryer sheet damage the book. After several days or weeks, the book should be taken out and allowed to air for several days before "test sniffing" it and placing in the hope chest.

Other items should be "sniffed," and you will need to decide if there is any odor, only a mild odor or if the smell is too strong to risk scenting the whole hope chest. But remember, once it is inside the chest, if the odor is too strong you may need treat every item inside to clear out the unwanted smell. Caution can once again prevent a future problem.

The third concern is dust. Even inside a hope chest, dust can be present and can cause damage by turning linens yellowish or dingy, taking the shine off of books and photos. This is easily avoided by placing as many items as possible, especially any linens, fabrics or clothing items, into linen or flannel storage bags or coverings. If the linen bags and coverings are all made from the same fabric, and if there is the same embroidery or monogramming on the bags, this can be another hidden gift for your daughter that will be a beautiful legacy for her and her children. When her children are grown she may bless each one with a linen bag from the set in her hope chest. This is something special that is easily done, it helps care for the items in the chest and will be treasured in the future.

Linen Bags

Although it may be very tempting to leave all the items loose inside the hope chest, so that with the very first glimpse as the lid is lifted there is awe, beauty and color everywhere you look, the items are not protected well and many mishaps can happen to the treasures that have taken time and effort to collect.

There are many reasons linen bags should be used. When an item is placed inside a linen bag, air is still able to flow through the material and allow the items to breathe, compare this to placing in plastic bags where there is no air movement and any moisture can lead to mold. The items can be neatly and carefully packed away, creating a very orderly look when the hope chest is opened. The linen bags also keep sets of linens, clothing, scrapbooks and their contents and photos or photo albums together. But the most important aspect of the linen bags is to prevent undo rubbing, scratching and snagging of items in the hope chest against each other or the sides of the chest. Although you and your daughter may not be continually going through the chest, every time something is moved about inside, it has the potential of causing snags, scratches or rubbing that can damage items.

Linen bags can easily be made and you do not need a great deal of sewing experience to attempt these. By adding lace, ribbons, embroidery or button closures you can make very beautiful and long-lasting bags to hold your daughter's treasures. If you are unable to make the bags yourself, or unable to find someone to do this for you, pillowcases can be used instead and can be decorated or left plain. The ends of the pillowcases can be secured in some fashion, with safety pins or ribbons, or carefully tucked underneath the item.

You can make the bags in any size you wish: large to fit quilts, small to fit special books, clothing items, jewelry and even larger ones to hold a family heirloom wedding gown. By making the bag to fit the item, you will be able to custom-make the whole set of linen bags. While she is young and learning to sew, allow your daughter to practice embroidery or other sewing on the linen bags, either with a specific design traced onto the fabric, or monogramming her initials in the center of each bag. This is very good practice and a wonderful start for preparing her hope chest for the items that will be placed within.

If your daughter is older, she can still practice embroidery quite easily on the linen bags, or she may want to decorate them using some other form of handiwork such as ribbon embroidery, quilting, crocheted or tatted lace or other embellishment.

The kinds of fabric used should have a high thread count, meaning that the fibers or threads in the fabric are so closely woven together there is very little or no space at all between them. The higher the thread count, the tighter the weave, and the better able to keep out dust and insects. High thread counts will also provide a longer wear or use time. The higher the thread count, the more fiber the threads will have to be worn and damaged before holes are formed. To find the thread count of linen, read the package carefully. Some manufacturers will have the thread count on the label of the item as well. You can also tell just by looking or touching the linen. A loose weave (low thread count) will have thicker threads that are father apart, often with knobby threads on the surface. A tight weave (higher thread count) will have thinner threads very close together and the surface will be smooth.

Keep in mind that although satins, silks and acrylics (polyester, rayon, etc.) may have a high thread count, these would not be good materials to protect from the rubbing, scratching and snagging that can happen within a hope chest. The fabric itself can easily be snagged and pulled on, causing holes to form in the bags. Silk is also not a good idea for long-term storage because it is made from the fibers of the silk worm. Silk begins to decompose and smell faster than a cotton fabric would.

Actual "linen" is the best to use but can be very expensive. Natural or bleached muslin or thick flannel are alternatives that will work nicely and be an economical alternative to the higher-cost linen fabric. Both are easy to work with and easy to embroider. Both should be pre-washed prior to making the bags, so any shrinkage will have taken place and there will be no worry that the finished and decorated bags will shrink further. When you have decided on the fabric you would like to use for the linen bags, consider purchasing a full bolt of fabric. This will allow you to make linen bags that match for many years to come. When you have finished a project, you can make a linen bag to place the item in. It's not uncommon to purchase small amounts of a fabric and then have trouble matching the fabric months and years later.

To make the simplest of the bags, you will basically be making the same thing as a pillowcase, only it will be made to fit a specific item. The thought is still the same however, three sides sewn closed with one side hemmed and left open. Some of the bags can be made with a drawstring opening. These would be good for small or irregular shaped items such as jewelry, small

toys or other small items. For larger bags, a button closure would be a better idea and would allow the bag to
lay flat, unlike the drawstring closure. This can be done
by taking the end opening and folding it back on itself,
then making several button holes along the length of
the bag where the flap sits. Attaching the buttons will
finish the bag. If you prefer to use ribbon to tie the bag
closed instead of buttons, this is another possibility.
And snaps or velcro would be still another option.

There is one more covering, traditionally called a
"linen cover". This is a very large cross-shaped piece of
fabric, like the plus sign in a math problem. All edges
have been turned under, and the item (usually a wedding gown) is folded and then placed in the center
square of the cross. The outer opposite sides of the cross
are then folded over, the last two opposite sides - having ribbons attached to them - tie the whole parcel
closed. The "linen cover" was often decorated with ribbon around the entire outer edge and a monogrammed
initial on the top flap. For the very wealthy, lavish embroidery would be sewn on the top flap.

Plastic Canvas Boxes and Containers

There is a multitude of patterns and booklets full of
instructions for making all kinds of small plastic canvas
boxes and circular containers. I have one pattern that
makes a 4" x 4" x 2" box with a monogrammed initial on
the top of the lid. Any of these boxes would make nice

storage containers for the hope chest, especially for smaller items that could easily get lost and fall to the bottom of the chest or fragile and easily-broken items.

Because each piece of plastic canvas has beautiful decorative sewing over the entire surface, it helps to keep out the dust as well as prevent the little box from damaging items in the chest. These boxes are very easy to make and come together quickly. You can match the threads used in the stitching to the colors you have used on your linen bags, to create a beautiful heirloom set.

At any fabric or craft store that sells plastic canvas, you will find at least a few booklets, for these containers. Some are very small and others quite large. There are directions for making almost anything you can think of, from dollhouse furniture and desktop accessories to needle cases and baby books! One of my favorite patterns is the old-fashioned Victorian Sewing Basket. When the "basket" is opened, the decorated sides lay flat to expose padded inside walls holding needles, thimbles, thread, small scissors and just about anything you would need for quick sewing or repairs. These were also commonly known as a "sailor's sewing kit."

Other Storage Containers

Small pressed cardboard boxes, often found in craft stores to use for decoupage and other projects, also make wonderful storage containers for the hope chest. You can find them in all sizes and shapes: small ones that would hold a few items of jewelry to large ones that could hold shoes. They come in all shapes, oval, circle, square, rectangle, stars, hexagons, hearts and more. These are relatively inexpensive and easily decorated, or they can even be left plain.

Consider decoupaging the box, using the same fabric you have used for the linen bags and embroidering a monogrammed initial on the fabric for the top. This will help match the box to the set of linen bags.

Boxes of all sorts can be used, whether decorated and matching, or not. If your chest does not have any drawers, boxes are a necessity. Children's smaller shoe boxes often work well, or metal tins leftover from Christmas cookies and candies. Anything that can be used, and has a lid, can be incorporated into the storage of items for the hope chest.

Packing the Hope Chest

Packing your chest will obviously vary, depending on the items you have chosen to put inside. There are several ways to go about this. What you need to keep in mind is to pack the heavier items on the bottom and the lighter ones on the very top. Breakables can be carefully wrapped in tissue paper for padding and placed between clothing and linen items. However, boxing the fragile items is the best insurance against breakage and would be the best option.

Packing the Chest

If you have a large amount of books, you may want to box them carefully, and place them somewhere outside the hope chest. Store them in a safe place, where they won't be exposed to water, heat or weather. This provides more room for smaller more fragile items in the hope chest. Special books, like a family Bible that is being handed down to your daughter, should be placed inside a linen bag made to fit, or an old clean pillowcase. This will allow a special book to be protected from rubbing and possibly page tears. It would also be a good idea to take the time to use tissue paper to wrap and pad those very old or precious books, and place them either in a cardboard box inside the hope chest or in a top tray of the chest. If they are placed at the bottom of the chest, without added protection from a box, there is the chance that over time they will shift and you will end up with a book that is slanted at the spine or has even been torn along the spine from the weight of the other items pressing on or against it.

If you will be storing china or other breakables in cardboard boxes or other containers outside of the hope chest, you should wrap them carefully in several layers of tissue paper and a final layer of bubble wrap. The extra precaution can help prevent any chipping and cracking if the box is bumped at all, or something falls on top of the box. When breakable items are stored long term, there is always the risk that someone will forget what the box contains and the items will become damaged. *label* the box carefully, with the words "Fragile" or

The Hope Chest

"China" on all sides as an additional safeguard.

If you are able to find bright red or yellow packing tape, or a similar tape, wrap it around the box several times. I have even gone so far as to write "Warning! Breakables!" on the tape, or to tape brightly-colored sheets of paper on the top of the box and write the warning on the paper. This has helped my husband know not to stack anything heavy on those boxes and to move them carefully.

Large or thick scrapbooks can be confined by wrapping all the way around with a large three inch ribbon, and tied to prevent items from falling out or pages being torn out accidentally. If the book is especially heavy or there are many loose items inside, criss-crossing with the wide ribbon, like wrapping a large present should provide more protection. Scrapbooks, after tying with ribbon, can also be placed inside a clean pillowcase or linen bag made to size, to keep dust off and also to keep the contents inside safe. One extra protection is to take acid-free tissue paper and place between each and every page to keep papers, pictures and photos from sticking together, especially if you will be storing the scrapbook for a long time.

Any audios or videos that you include should be individually placed inside sealable plastic bags, especially if you do not have the original plastic cases to place them in. This is probably the one area where the "no plastic in the hope chest" policy would be allowed. The plastic will help to prevent dust or moisture from causing damage and keep lint from getting inside the tapes from any fabric items they may rub against. The tape's plastic case will also afford a small amount of protection against physical damage. You can bubble wrap the tape and place it in a sealable plastic bag if you do not have a case for the tape. It would be a good idea to place these tapes into a small box, or if you have a top tray or drawers in the hope chest, this would also be a good place for them.

Loose photos, especially old ones, should have a piece of acid-free paper or acid-free tissue paper placed between each and every photo to prevent them from sticking to each other. The photos should then be placed into a shallow box to be stored in the chest. Photo albums that do not have sheet protectors should also have acid-free paper or acid-free tissue paper placed between each page, and then tied in the same way as the scrapbooks to prevent the photographs from sticking together or falling out. Both the boxed photos or the photo album should be placed within a linen bag or clean pillowcase. These should be taken out and checked at least once a year, especially if there is any doubt that some of the pictures are damp or show signs of mold or mildew. Mold and mildew spores can still continue to grow slowly and destroy old photographs if not caught in time, even if there is little or no moisture present. Those old photographs you have recently found, or an elderly relative may have given you, could be harboring mold spores that you can't see. If you have only recently received the photos, or are unsure just where and how they had previously been stored, it's a good idea to check them every few months for a year or two so you can catch any mildew that might start up in their new environment.

If you should find any mold forming on your old photos, you may want to contact a company that restores old photographs for help. Once the mold begins to form on the paper, it is very hard to stop it unless you have professional help, and there is the possibility it will spread to all of your other photographs as well as books and fabrics.

Special linens, such as a quilt or handmade afghan, should be carefully folded with the back side of the quilt showing, to protect the top of the quilt. These items should also be placed in a linen bag or cover made to the right size, to prevent dust and rubbing damage. Other linens, such as embroidered sheets and pillowcases, should all be folded to the same size and placed as sets or groups into a linen bag as well. A pretty ribbon tied around the little stack to hold them all together is a pleasant way to "set them aside for the future". This also allows you to easily stack the little bundles and move items around inside the chest without sets being misplaced, damaged, unfolded and wrinkled or becoming dirty from handling.

If you have a wedding dress and veil, a christening gown, a bridal set made for the wedding night or any special piece of clothing, it would be very prudent to take the time to make a special linen bag or linen covering to place that special clothing item in. If you are unable to make a linen bag, then do try to find a sturdy box to place the special item in.

Chest Designs and Adding Accessories

There are a few alternatives to the basic plain chest, and these can be added to a chest that is an heirloom or has been purchased through a store. The most common addition would be to place wood runners along the inside of the front and back side pieces of the chest and to make small drawers to sit on top of the runners. This is fairly easy and would allow the drawers to be moved back and forth, and also to be lifted in and out for more accessibility to the items below.

Another alternative is to make a "shelf," with several legs. You would be able to place heavy items, or breakable items, on the floor of the chest, and then place the "shelf" over the items. The legs of the shelf would be standing on the chest floor, supporting the shelf, keeping weight off of the items beneath it. It works on the same idea as a pie or cake "safe." The bottom pie or cake sits on the bottom of the "safe," with multiple pies and cakes above it on shelves or racks that have legs supporting each new layer. The shelf itself can be made of pressboard, plywood or pegboard (to allow better ventilation in the chest). It should be made slightly smaller than the inner dimensions of the chest and should have at least one cross-piece across the middle of the shelf for support. It would also be best not to place heavy items over the middle of the shelf, but balance the weight evenly. If there was a need for heavy items to be placed on the shelf, consider using 1/2 inch plywood or putting a leg support under the middle of the shelf. This is actually a very easy alternative to make, and several "shelves" can be placed inside the same chest. If you will be storing a large number of breakable items, such as china or crystal, it would be a very good idea to invest the effort and time to make these "shelves" for the chest.

Perfume, Essential Oils and Cedar Wood

Brief and fleeting scents are often incredible memory triggers. With the faintest whiff, memories of people we have known and loved, places we have been to, things we have seen and enjoyed, come flooding back to us. Fragrance, odors, scents, smells...they bind images and memories to us in a physical, intangible way. A hope chest, like other familiar places and things, has a special memory link through the aromas that storage and time have accumulated.

It is an unusual person who does not enjoy opening her hope chest to have a very special and unique fragrance greet her. Some chests are enhanced by the owner placing a particular fragrance inside to permeate the chest. Other chests are left to absorb the natural aroma of the items placed inside. Some people choose to place cedar lining around the inner walls of their chest, or to use cedar balls throughout, which leaves its own particular fragrance. This is a personal choice and one you should think about carefully before you make a decision. Once you decide to put a perfume inside the chest, there is no way to retrieve it. The aroma will forever haunt the hope chest with its fragrance.

If you decide to place a special perfume inside, or to use cedar lining or balls, there are several precautions you should be aware of. Whichever fragrance you choose, it will permeate the interior of the hope chest for life. So choose very carefully.

The most common choice is an actual perfume. Place several cotton balls inside a small jar that has been washed and dried thoroughly. Place the perfume liberally onto the cotton balls until slightly damp. Do not overly wet the cotton balls or you will have moisture inside the chest and the scent will be far too strong. You can use old stockings or a loose weave fabric across the opening of the jar and secure it around the rim of the jar with a rubber band or ribbon to keep the cotton balls in place. The jar is then placed inside the hope chest where it will not tip over. The best placement for the jar is in a corner of a top tray where there is ample air movement. If that is not possible, place the jar within the depths of the hope chest, but use care so the cotton balls will not fall out and possibly damage any items. As the perfume evaporates into the chest, it will permeate everything within. Once the cotton balls are dry, usually within a few days to a week, you may take them out or leave them in for future use.

Although the fragrance will last a long time, it will slowly weaken over the years, especially after the original application. A fresh application of perfume will help enhance the fragrance again. You may not need to reapply the perfume for several months or perhaps years, depending on how often you open the chest. Be aware however that if you choose an actual perfume, it may one day be out of production and you will not be able to re-apply the fragrance. Purchasing a full bottle will allow your daughter to refresh the fragrance as needed, even when she is a great-grandmother. This goes for essential oils as well. You may want to purchase several of the small bottles in case the oil ever goes out of production. Essential oils often have a very strong fragrance to start, and then they peter out quickly. Having extra on hand is a definite must!

You should never at any time spritz perfume or oil directly onto the contents of the hope chest or onto the wood itself. This can cause the wood or items to stain, or cause damage to the articles that come in contact with the misting spray. Instead of spritzing, the safest way to impart the fragrance is using the cotton ball method mentioned above.

Take care that nothing is allowed to block the top of the jar, so the air can flow around it and throughout the rest of the chest. Refresh the cotton balls every six months or so for the first few years or until the fragrance begins to become a steady and permanent part of the hope chest. Depending on how full the hope chest is, the strength of the fragrance, and the length of time you have had the perfume or oil inside, the fragrance will take hold and slowly sink into the articles and the wood itself. After many years, the fragrance will have a deeper subtle strength to it, and you will not need to refresh it as often.

The choice of perfume or essential oil should be given solely to your daughter who will be the owner of the hope chest at some point. A mother may prefer a different fragrance over her daughter's choice, but remember that once the fragrance is in the hope chest, you can assume it will be there for life. The choice should rest with your daughter.

If you are not pleased with her choice, or she had a hard time deciding on a fragrance, or perhaps you feel she may change her mind within a few months or even a year or two...there is no reason to hurry with the decision. Allow her to sample many different fragrances over a period of time, and if need be re-sample over and over for several years. This decision should not be rushed, but it should be carefully weighed and a final decision made when she is ready. Allow your daughter to mature, let her tastes and choices mature, and when she is ready you can purchase what her choice is.

It may be a pleasant surprise for your daughter if you were to take her "unknowingly" to the department store as a fun "mother-daughter" time to window shop and enjoy each other. While you are there, experiment with the different perfumes. Mentally take notes of which fragrances she prefers, and which ones she really disliked. In several months do this once more, and see if her preferences have changed. If so, plan on doing it again in the future until she has settled onto one particular fragrance that she seems to prefer over all others. When you feel she has really and truly decided on just one that she prefers, you can purchase it for her as a gift for her hope chest. You can either present it to her at that time, or keep the surprise a bit longer.

If you keep the surprise, secretly place a few drops onto the cotton balls in the jar and place it into her hope chest when she is occupied elsewhere. The next time she opens her hope chest to place something inside, she will be pleasantly surprised by the fragrance wafting out to greet her and by your happy little secret.

An added gift, especially if she is fond of one specific fragrance, would be to purchase a bottle of the perfume that she can use when she becomes engaged and on her wedding day. If she is frugal, she can make that one little bottle last a very long time. On successive wedding anniversaries, she can dab a little of that special perfume on, and have wonderful memories surround her. It will undoubtedly remind her dear husband of their special day as well...a very sweet and special link that the two of them can share.

Packing the Chest

My oldest sister was given a special bottle of perfume by her fiancée shortly after their engagement was announced. He had secretly picked it out himself, and told her the fragrance reminded him of her sweetness and her love. It was a special gift between the two of them, and no one really knew about it. She wore it during the wedding rehearsal, and again on their wedding day. She also wore it on special occasions and on their anniversaries. When they would have one of their rare disagreements, she would wear that special perfume to bed, letting her husband know that she loved him very much. When each of her three children was born, she would take that same little bottle to the hospital with her, and put a little perfume on before labor got too heavy. She wanted her babies' first smell to be of that special perfume. I know it sounds silly, but I have been a little envious of her perfume ever since she told me about this several years ago.

Julie W, Chicago

Essential oils are often less expensive than good - quality perfume. If you plan on using essential oil in the hope chest, experiment to find which one your daughter prefers. You can use the oil in her clothes closet, her dresser or in a linen closet where you store sheets and towels. Some oils may change their aroma slightly with age, so it's best to use it first and make sure you enjoy it before placing it in the hope chest.

There are two kinds of essential oils that have a

cedar fragrance: the first is a Canadian essential oil called "Canadian Red Cedar - *Cedrus Canadiensis*" and sold in British Columbia Canada. The United States version is "Cedar Wood - *Cedrus Atlantica*" and sold throughout the U.S.

In my own chest, I have a very small jar of perfume that someone gave me as a child, and it was in a solid paste form. It was meant to be rubbed onto the skin instead of sprayed. This was a pleasant fragrance, and I did not need to worry about it spilling in my hope chest. I used a rubber band to secure a piece of polyester netting onto the top, and it has been inside the corner of my top tray ever since. The solid part of the perfume has dried out, shrunken and cracked over the years, but it still has a wonderful fragrance that I enjoy every time I open my hope chest.

I would like to stress that there is NO hurry in picking out a fragrance to be placed inside the hope chest. And there may be mothers and daughters who would rather not have a fragrance in their hope chest at all, but instead have that "old antique flavor" to the interior from the many different articles and items being placed closely together for a long period of time. There may be allergies that need to be considered as well. So for each family the choice will be different and unique, just like the vast and distinct selection of items placed inside each hope chest.

Cedar

The Hope Chest

Chapter Sixteen
Will It Be a Surprise?

You have decided to begin collecting many wonderful and special treasures that you can set aside for your daughter in her hope chest. You have prayed about what to save, collect, buy or make to form a very unique and personal gift for her. Now comes the hard part...will everything that goes inside the hope chest be a secret until she is grown and married, or will you let her help you choose and decide what goes inside?

Decisions! But there is something you should carefully consider. If she knows about each and every item, she can help you place things in her hope chest that she would like to have. She can also help you with collecting the information and history that goes with each item and all the memories involved in creating her hope chest. Your daughter can let you know if she wants something saved or not. This could be a tie-that-binds a mother and daughter together and builds a deeper love and appreciation for one another.

During those often unpredictable and emotional teen years, it can also be used as an encouragement to

The Hope Chest

keep her pure, to keep her mind set on the future and to help encourage her to learn the skills she will need as a wife and mother. There is a great reward from working with our hands, and part of that reward is seeing the items you have made grow and build up in your hope chest until it is full and even overflowing...this comes from personal experience as well as from talking with others who have had their own hope chests.

I have begun to think more seriously about a Hope Chest for my daughter. So...when I was at Barnes and Noble I saw a discounted book on napkin folding and decided to purchase this for my daughter, Amanda. I bought it with the intentions of tucking it away to put in her Hope Chest. BUT, I just couldn't do it. I showed her the book and she was so excited. I bought her a set of napkins from the thrift store and she has truly enjoyed experimenting with these. We have had fun together making memories...and she even took them to one of my friend's house and spent some time with her folding napkins. I feel it is important to purchase things that you will use together...so that she takes a chest of memories with her as well as useful items.

I do think it will be special for her to pull out little surprises as she unpacks her chest, but it will be even more special as she spends time remembering the precious times we had

Cindy McCarthy

Will It Be a Surprise?

Knowing about the treasures set aside for her when she marries one day can be a strong and physical tie that will keep her mind and body on the course she knows is right, and you have set in place for her. Every time she sees her hope chest, every time she places another item or handmade article within, it will be a constant reminder of what is expected of her and can also be a very strong and physical encouragement for her heart and mind.

Your daughter's hope chest is a very "physical" reward for all her hard work and effort at learning the skills she will one day need to know, and it is a continual reminder of the love her parents have for her. It is not unreasonable to let her go through her hope chest when she feels a need to do so. She is dreaming her dreams of the future, and this allows her mind and heart to communicate and can give her the strength to follow where God is leading her. It gives her a strong foundation to stand on, and one that is continually being rewarded by each and every item that is placed inside.

On the other hand, keeping a few special items set aside for her that she knows are in the chest, hidden in linen bags that have been sewn closed until her wedding day, would be a wonderful surprise waiting for her. You might also like to keep several items for her in secret, to give her as a gift when she becomes engaged or for her wedding. It can also keep her interest mounting in preparing her hope chest and in her future.

The Hope Chest

There is nothing more irresistible than a secret, especially when that secret has a unknown date in the future for it to be revealed. This is an inventive way of keeping her mind on her hope chest and encouraging her to continue to practice skills and place items inside. To have a secret waiting for her to be revealed on her wedding day, with special items that have been waiting for years to be opened...this is a tantalizing treat.

If you do not think your daughter would appreciate having items in her hope chest that she can't see for years to come, or that her curiosity would be too unbearable for her, you can always secretly set them aside for her somewhere else to be brought out for her wedding day.

If you have an extra-special item you would like to make sure is set aside for a specific daughter, consider placing it inside a finished linen bag and sewing the opening closed. Label it in some way, and place the item in her hope chest. This will insure that the right daughter receives her item and there will be no mix-up.

> Just recently I was helping my dear, sweet mother-in-law finally go through "her" mother's things in Nannie's cedar chest. I treasured Nannie. She was a very special lady. The day that we went through her chest, we found several sets of hand worked dresser scarves, baby sets that belonged to my mother-in-law and my dear husband too, and beautiful hand-embroidered sets of matching pillowcases.

Will It Be a Surprise?

There were enough there for me to put back a set for each of my five children. They don't know about these. I've wrapped them up and plan on presenting these to my daughters, and my boys too, when we begin to "stock" their hope chests.

Over the years Nannie had given me several sets, including a set for our wedding which I still use 26 years later. I can't wait to see the faces of our children when they realize that they have a present from their own Nannie. And I think, for me, that *that* is one of the primary reasons for our hope chests- to provide for our children's future homes with links from the past.

Does that seem unlikely through just a set of pillowcases? I think not. Because every time I use a set that she made for me, I find myself stroking it as I place the pillow inside, remembering her sweet spirit, her love for the Lord, and her love for her family. And *that's* why each child will find a pair of Nannie's pillowcases in their hope chest, whether it is a real chest, as in my girls' instances, or a figurative one for my boys."

Merri Williams, GA

And how about the final thought of keeping ALL the items you have set aside for her to be completely secret, and opened only when she is married? This indeed would be a hard thing for a mother to do and for a daughter to bear. I have yet to meet any mother who would consider this last suggestion, though there may be some out there. But this would truly have to be something that had special circumstances attached to it, and I will list only a few in case there are parents who may be helped and encouraged by this idea.

If there has been a recent death in the family of someone very dear to your daughter's heart, and she has been given many items that could be the beginning of a hope chest for her, but these items would bring her to tears if she were to know of them so immediately after the death of that special person...this too would be a reason to keep them secret until she has worked through her grief and can look at the items and see the love that was intended to be shown in her new possessions... not the fresh heartache that would leave sad memories linked to those items for life. When she is ready, it will be a deep inner blessing for her to receive, in love, the items that once belonged to someone she cared very deeply about.

If your daughter has absolutely *no* interest in a hope chest, now that you would like to start preparing one for her, this would be a good time to quietly begin setting items inside her hope chest or a closet. Do not be discouraged! Children go through different stages and have differing items that are close to their heart. It may be that she is just not at the point where these things matter to her. Whether she takes an active interest in making items or not, at some point in her future she will look back and see her childhood memories in the hope chest and the articles her parents saved for her.

Will It Be a Surprise?

If there is a family crisis going on, or your daughter has a severe medical or psychological problem, you will have to decide whether it would benefit her to help with the creation of her hope chest or make her more depressed. Pray and follow the Lord's leading, I have no doubt in my heart that He will answer you here in this situation.

I was given my hope chest for my thirteenth birthday, which was shortly after my older brother was critically injured and comatose for several months. I consider the gift of my hope chest to be the one thing in all those terrible times that allowed me to think beyond what was happening in my immediate life, and it allowed me put all my energies and my heart into something hopeful. My hope chest allowed me to plan and dream of the future, and prepare for a life of happiness when all around me my family was in turmoil and pain. It was the one thing that allowed me to start living again.

These are only a few examples, and don't underestimate what a simple box can do...with prayer, the Lord can show parents what, where, how and when to prepare their daughter's hope chest and what will be a blessing for their precious daughter.

When Is It Your Daughter's Chest?

The hope chest you are creating for your daughter belongs to her from the very moment the thought enters your heart and your mind, until it is physically given to her. This may differ slightly for each family. Both parents should discuss this, and a decision needs to be made on what would be the appropriate time for giving your daughter the physical possession of her hope chest.

Most parents will give their daughter her hope chest when the wooden chest has been built or bought and allow her to fill it with their help and supervision, all the while it is in her sole possession.

Some parents may want to allow their daughter to have partial custody of the hope chest, allowing her to place items inside and go through its contents whenever she wishes, but still keeping a hand involved in what is kept inside until it is completely relinquished into her care on the day she marries.

Some may wish to keep the hope chest in the care and control of the parents and allow their daughter to take peeks and place items she has made inside, with the understanding that at a certain point it will be given to her to keep as her own. Her engagement or her wedding day would probably be a good time.

There are any number of ways this can be worked out, and each family needs to find the way that will work best for them. The most important aspect in this area is to have both parents agree and stand by that agreement unless circumstances alter it.

Will It Be a Surprise?

My Daddy is a retired farmer and furniture maker. He has made over 150 Hope Chests, four of which are in our house. He made one for me to hold my girls' "growing up memories" and one for each of our girls to use as hope chests.

My hope chest was an antique trunk that belonged to my great-great-Aunt Verdi. I no longer have the trunk, but I do have memories of filling it with wonderful treasures to use when I married.

The chests my Dad makes are pine on the outside with cedar lining, heavy, durable and just wonderful! My girls were 5, 6 and 7 when they received their chests.

Janet Skiles

Another 1880 embroidery monogram pattern to use.

The Hope Chest

Chapter Seventeen
In Closing...

It is my heartfelt hope that parents and children alike will have seeds planted in their hearts by reading this little book. Whether someone is blessed with an actual physical chest, or through the little items that have been saved and kept for them in a shoebox over many years, joy and happiness can still be found. It is not the physical "chest" or the money that has gone into the items that will make it special and unique...but the time, intention, and love that parents have for their child that will be the real gift. The hope chest is given from the heart, with no strings attached, and with very little money being spent. It can be one of the greatest gifts anyone can receive.

Each hope chest is totally unique and priceless. The actual preparation of the items created for chest will offer its own struggles, its own failures, its own triumphs. A hope chest will strengthen and enhance your daughter's character through her efforts and the work and skill of her hands and heart.

Although the hope chest may be full of material

The Hope Chest

possessions that will add beauty and charm to your daughter's future home, it will be the inner knowledge she takes with her that will be the true beauty.

Another 1880 embroidery monogram pattern to use.

In Closing...

The Hope Chest

Bibliography:

- Webster, Noah. American Dictionary of the English Language. Foundation for American Christian Education, 1995.

- Babys Pleasure Book, Copyright 1880

- Baldwin's Readers - Fifth Year. American Book Company, 1897

- Luke, Mary M. Catherine The Queen, 1971

- Funk & Wagnalls New Comprehensive International Dictionary of the English Language; Encyclopedic Edition. Ferguson Publishing Company, 1978.

- Funk, Wilfred. Funk & Wagnalls Stand Reference Encyclopedia, 1958.

- King James Bible
-
- Eichler, Lillian. The New Book of Etiquette by Lillian Eichler. Nelson Doubleday Inc., 1924.

- McPharlin, Paul. Love and Courtship in America Paul McPharlin. Hasting House, Publishers Inc., 1946.

- Treat, E. B. Mother, Home & Heaven, 1878.

- Needlecraft Magazine, January. 1925.

- Young, John. Our Deportment. Pennsylvania Publishing Co., 1880

- The Hope Chest. H. E. Verran Company Inc., 1917.

- Bowman, Loreen and Kift, jane Leslie. The Hope Chest: A Book for the Bride. The Reilly and Lee Company, 1922.

- Polacco, Patricia. The Keeping Quilt. Simon and Schuster Books for Young People, 1988.

- What a Young Wife Ought to Know, 1908

The Hope Chest
Appendix:

- The Keeping Quilt by Patricia Polacco

- Mary Frances Sewing Book by Jane Eayre Fryer

- Mary Frances Garden Book by Jane Eayre Fryer

- Mary Frances Knitting & Crocheting Book by Jane Eayre Fryer

- The Hope Chest: A Book for the Bride by Lorene Bowman & Jane Kift (reprinted through Hope Chest Legacy)

- The Boy Joiner by Ellis Davidson (soon to be reprinted through Hope Chest Legacy)

- Spencerian Handwriting Theory & Copy Books

- Training Our Daughters to be Keepers at Home by Mrs. Craig (Ann) Ward

- Beautiful Girlhood by Mabel Hale

- Only a Servant by Kristina Roy

- The Hope Cheat by H. A. Verran booklet (reprinted through Hope Chest Legacy)

Pre-Made & Made-To-Order Hope Chests:

Hope Chest Legacy
(888) 554-7292
http://www.HopeChestLegacy.com
Email: HopeChestLegacy@aol.com
Offering hope chest building plans and pre-cut kits.

Kentucky Hills Cedar
(270)433-5710
http://www.kyhillscedar.com
email: truecrew@duo-county.com
Offering handmade hope chests from a variety of woods.

Recommended Catalogs, Magazines and Companies:

Creative Needle Magazine
1 Apollo Rd., Lookout Mtn., GA 30750
(706) 820-2600
email: info@creativeneedlemag.com

Friends Patterns (Amish-Mennonite clothing patterns)
PO Box 657
Berthoud, CO. 80513-0657

The Hope Chest

Hope Chest Legacy
PO Box 1398, Littlerock, CA. 93543
(888) 554-7292
HopeChestLegacy@aol.com - or - www.HopeChestLegacy.com

Herrschners Inc.
2800 Hoover Road
Stevens Point, WI 54492
1-800-441-0838   fax 1-715-341-2250
http://www.herrschners.com/
email: Herrschners.comFAQ

Rod & Staff Publishers
(offers wonderful coloring books that are good for tracing patterns
 onto fabric for embroidery)
P.O. Box 3 Hwy. 172 Crockett, Kentucky 41413-0003 USA
(606)-522-4348 Fax (800)-643-1244
http://anabaptists.org/ras/

Sew Baby:
313 N. Mattis Ave #116
Champaign, IL. 61821
1-800-249-1907
http://www.sewbaby.com

Sew Beautiful Magazine
  (Embroidery, Women & Children, Classic Heirlooms)
Sew Beautiful Subscription Dept.
149 Old Big Cove Rd, Brownsboro, AL 36741-9985
(256) 534-5200
email: editorial@marthapullen.com
http://www.marthapullen.com

Spencerian Handwriting Theory & Copy Books
Mott Media
112 E. Ellen Street
Fenton, MI. 48430
(800) 421-6645 (for orders only)
(810) 714-4280 (for other inquiries)
http://mottmedia.com/spencer.html

The Nordic Needle (Specializes in Fine Needlework)
1314 Gateway Dr. SW
Fargo, ND 58103
(701) 235-5231   fax (701) 235-0952
http://www.nordicneedle.com
email: infor@nordicneedle.com

Classic Quilting & Design (Machine Quilting for Quilt Tops)
(661) 285-9242
http://www.quiltingdesigns.com
email: qdesigns@qnet.com
(you may be able to find this type of service in your local area through the phone
book, look under machine quilting or ask at your local fabric store)

Internet Used Book Sites:

(Find OOP books)

Bookfinder
http://www.bookfinder.com

ebay (auction house, out-of-print books up for auction daily)
http://www.ebay.com

Bibliofind
hhtp://www.bibliofind.com

Alibris
http://www.alibris.com

Online Support and Email Groups:

www.HopeChestLegacy.com
HopeChestLegacy@aol.com
Hope-Chest-Legacy-subscribe@yahoogroups.com

We always enjoy hearing from our readers!
Please drop us a note with your comments,
questions, stories or experiences...

Email Rebekah Wilson at:
www.HopeChestLegacy.com

NOTES...

NOTES...

NOTES...

NOTES...

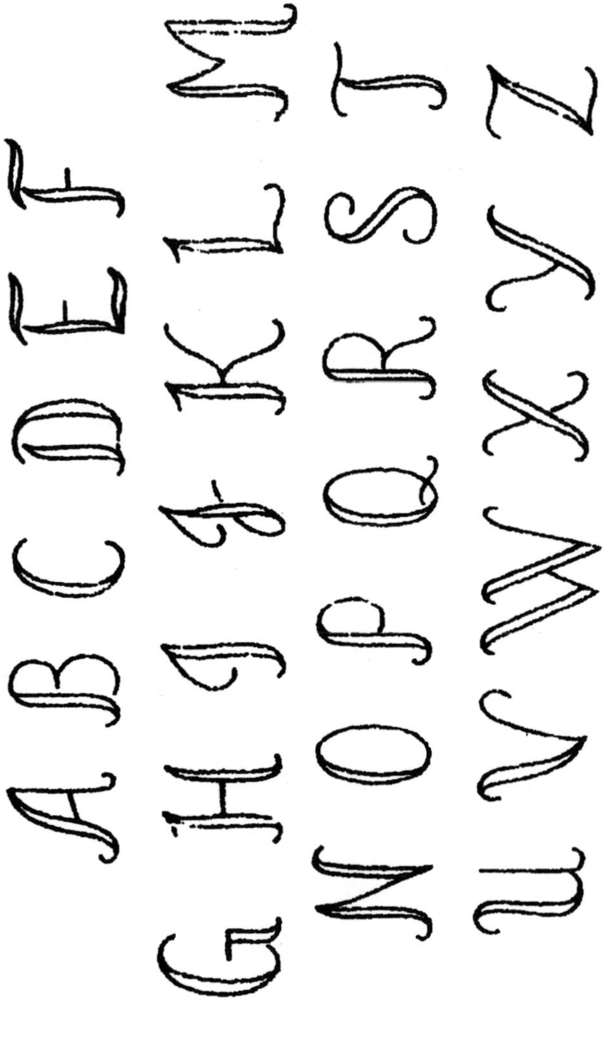
A B C D E F
G H I J K L M
N O P Q R S T
U V W X Y Z